A GUIDE TO
MEDIEVAL
GARDENS

GARDENS IN THE AGE OF CHIVALRY

A GUIDE TO
MEDIEVAL GARDENS

GARDENS IN THE AGE OF CHIVALRY

MICHAEL BROWN

WHITE OWL

AN IMPRINT OF PEN & SWORD BOOKS LTD.
YORKSHIRE – PHILADELPHIA

First published in Great Britain in 2022 by
White Owl
An imprint of
Pen & Sword Books Ltd
Yorkshire - Philadelphia

ISBN 978 1 52679 454 3

Typeset in 11/14 pts Cormorant Infant
by SJmagic DESIGN SERVICES, India.

Printed and bound in India by Replika Press Pvt. Ltd.

Pen & Sword Books Ltd incorporates the imprints of Pen & Sword Books Archaeology, Atlas, Aviation, Battleground, Discovery, Family History, History, Maritime, Military, Naval, Politics, Railways, Select, Transport, True Crime, Fiction, Frontline Books, Leo Cooper, Praetorian Press, Seaforth Publishing, Wharncliffe and White Owl.

For a complete list of Pen & Sword titles please contact

PEN & SWORD BOOKS LIMITED
47 Church Street, Barnsley, South Yorkshire, S70 2AS, England
E-mail: enquiries@pen-and-sword.co.uk
Website: www.pen-and-sword.co.uk

or

PEN AND SWORD BOOKS
1950 Lawrence Rd, Havertown, PA 19083, USA
E-mail: Uspen-and-sword@casematepublishers.com
Website: www.penandswordbooks.com

Contents

Introduction

I began work on the medieval gardens at the Prebendal Manor, Nassington, in late 1995. The house is the longest continually inhabited house in Northamptonshire and the twenty-fifth such building in Britain. A prebendary is a canon, a member of the clergy who is on the staff of a cathedral church, in this particular case Lincoln Cathedral. The prebendary at Nassington had a seat that can still be seen in the choir of Lincoln Cathedral. Above this seat are written the psalms that the prebendary was supposed to say every day. In reality the prebendary usually paid a poor priest to do this for him. A prebend is the manor that was the living of the prebendary; somewhere to live and earn him an income. Each prebendary was meant to only have one prebend, but this was not always the case.

I decided to create a garden based on those of the time of Nicholas Colnet, one of the prebendaries of the manor, who had at least one other manor elsewhere. Colnet had been physician for Henry V, accompanying him on what we now know as the Agincourt campaign. Colnet received the manor in 1417, possibly for services rendered. Archaeology has not so far been able to discover any gardens that may have belonged to him, so I decided to create high status garden features and to grow the plants that we know were in use for medicines and pleasure during the early fifteenth century. Originally I had only intended it to be a small trellis-enclosed garden with a fountain and a turf seat, but very soon enthusiasm took over and the garden became the largest medieval-style garden in Europe, with a tunnel arbour, a tree seat, a tree arbour, a vineyard, vegetable garden and coppice. Later, more decorative areas were added. In his book based on the BBC 1 series, 'Royal Gardeners', Alan Titchmarsh described the gardens as: 'A stunning example of a recreated medieval garden.'

This book contains a fraction of the years of research that I carried out on medieval gardens, their plants and their uses, medieval food, agricultural crops, animal management and the medieval period in general. I studied medieval herbals, trawled through archaeology reports, visited records offices and have made translations of original documents. It would be more than any one lifetime's work to go through all the original documents, so I have been grateful to follow others and to add my own work and ideas. The book contains a general outline of the plants that were grown in medieval gardens. I hope that a book about the uses of medieval plants will be published in the near future to complement this book.

✻✻✻✻✻

It is a beautiful summer day. The sky is a clear, deep blue. Birds sing in the trees. Doves drink at a bubbling fountain. Insects hum and the air is heavy with the scent of lilies and roses.

Finely dressed ladies sit on the grass or seats, making rose circlets for their heads. Instruments are playing. Melodious voices sing in harmony. People are dancing in the shade of the trees. Some are reading books; others discuss love as they sip wine. It is

Doves added beauty to a garden but were also bred for food.

the perfect medieval day, in the perfect medieval garden. But just how true are the medieval images showing the elites enjoying the luxuries of life? Was it all just wishful thinking?

Medieval gardens occupy the most ephemeral period of European garden history. The sites of many such gardens have been recorded, but little information on the layout, or the selection of the plants and how they were arranged has been confirmed by archaeological excavation. As a result, we are left with the more tenuous evidence that is provided by poetry, tapestries, illuminated manuscripts and financial accounts for information on the possible appearance and planting of a medieval garden. Although these sources give us many clues regarding the likely appearance of high-status medieval gardens, we have little hard historical fact. Gardens for pleasure may not have been very common, especially in the earlier medieval period, but they certainly existed, if only for the wealthy, but their appearance can only ever be informed imagination.

CHAPTER 1

Evidence of Medieval Gardens

Most of the illustrations of medieval gardens date from the fourteenth century and were not painted in England, so if we are specifically researching pictorial evidence for British medieval gardens we have very little to work from. There are only two surviving pictures that were painted in England showing such garden scenes.

A couple playing a form of backgammon in a sunken turf seat. (Wiki Commons)

One is of a turf seat in the *Luttrel Psalter*. The manuscript was made for the Luttrell family, who lived in the village of Ingham, Lincolnshire and dates from 1325–1340. It is a book of psalms that shows many scenes of daily life of the period. This includes an isolated scene of a crowned man and a woman playing backgammon in a turf seat that, unusually, appears to be sunk into the ground.

The other English garden picture shows a king and queen sitting on a raised turf seat, playing a chess-like board game in a small garden area within a garden next to a castle. The turf is full of flowers and beyond the paling fence a gardener is pruning a tree with a billhook.

Tapestries

A proper woven tapestry for the wall was something that only the very wealthy could afford. If you had less money, you would have a sheet of linen painted to look as if it were a tapestry. Tapestries often show scenes with symbolic meaning, religious and otherwise, such as the *Hunt of the Unicorn*. Many tapestries show plants and idealised landscapes. The most useful sources for plants are the *Mille-Fleurs* tapestries, literally meaning thousands of flowers. Many of the flowers are true to life and are easily identified. As with illuminated manuscripts, the tapestries that have survived were mostly made on the European mainland and reflect the European local plants. The pictures do not always show plants realistically, and even when they do, the plants are usually shown as all being in flower at the same time, a pretty touch of artistic licence.

So how reliable are European pictures as a guide to English medieval gardens? The culture of chivalry was common to most of Europe, and the European ruling elite generally aspired to the same ideals. To some extent these ideals were encouraged by the church, possibly as an attempt to civilise the constantly bickering and fighting ruling classes. The church became instrumental in the preparation of a knight, who was expected to keep a vigil during the night before his knighting ceremony. The accoutrements of a knight became associated with Christian ideals, as did his duties to protect women, children and the poor. Unfortunately, the reality of life was another matter entirely. The wealthy endowed land and money to the church, and had chapels built in their own homes or in their parish church. Secular lords and ladies would have their personal religious books to contemplate. These Breviaries and Psalters usually contained lavish paintings of biblical scenes in medieval settings, complete with buildings and gardens, reflecting their owners' hopes and dreams. The secular aspirations of chivalry were also promoted through the arts. The popular Romances told stories of knights, love and fighting; and just like us, the ruling classes loved to hear tales of how they thought their lives ought to be. A delightful garden was something that many of the wealthy would aspire to owning, and a peaceful place to enjoy their leisure time.

Use of Estate Accounts

The pictorial evidence and that suggested by poetry and literature can be confirmed to some extent by studying estate expenses. Records of the money paid for labour and materials support the idea that real gardens closely matched those depicted in the arts, and they can offer us a few glimpses of medieval horticulture. The cost of repair work tells us what was being repaired, whether garden features or buildings within it. Garden walls, doors and the locks for them are frequently referred to. Tools were bought or repaired, and inventories often list the cost of the tools and equipment that belonged to the landowner.

Physical Evidence of Medieval Gardens

Until recently, archaeology was more interested in buildings than the gardens that accompanied them and much evidence was casually destroyed. Thankfully, archaeologists are now more sympathetic to the full picture of life in the past. One area of research that may bring results in the future is the relatively recent discipline of environmental archaeology. This is the study of soil samples taken from stratified features to detect pollen, surviving seeds or even plant material. Most organic material can survive for centuries in waterlogged deposits such as in ditches and ponds. There have even been cases of seeds surviving in the thatch of medieval buildings. Seeds that have been charred by fire, intentionally as in cookery or otherwise also tend to survive. Unfortunately, most of this evidence tends to be from woody material such as nuts, fruit stones and pips, or the larger cornfield weed seeds, such as *Agrostemma githago*, corncockle, and charred grains.

At the Prebendal Manor, Northamptonshire, soil analysis from an Anglo-Saxon beam slot in a building showed that there were two seeds of the Caryophyllaceae family, the cultivated *Dianthus*, commonly known as pinks, which were most likely to have been intentionally cultivated. There were more seeds in soil samples taken from other areas of the site. They were what we now consider to be weeds: three vetch seeds, two dock seeds and one seed of fat hen, although seeds and leaves of fat hen were used as food in the past. Other soil samples contained many grain seeds, including emmer wheat, bread wheat, rye, oats and naked barley, along with beans and peas which were another part of the early staple diet.

The Castle Studies Trust has undertaken a project in Ireland to research the plants growing among the ruins and the land around four castles to try to establish which plants may have been grown.

Pollen analysis offers further clues to the plants that grew in the vicinity. Important information has been discovered about landscapes from pollen samples, but they are of limited use when it comes to gardens. Pollen is very tiny and light, making it easily carried for considerable distances by even a soft breeze, so while we may gain information about certain plants growing locally, this does not confirm that the plants were intentionally grown in a garden. There is another dilemma: even if it is possible to prove that the plants were growing in a garden, the evidence offers no clues as to how the plants were arranged, which makes a great difference to how the garden could have appeared to people visiting at the time.

Non-invasive techniques such as ground radar and other geo-physical methods can detect different features in the ground without the need to disturb the soil. These methods are especially good for later gardens where there may be the remains of garden walls, buildings and other large structures, but as yet, these methods have not fully confirmed the existence of earlier medieval gardens. The problem is that the smaller enclosed medieval gardens may only leave a few traces in the soil, such as the holes from wattle fencing and the pegs to hold raised beds in place. There be some foundation remains of a stone turf bench or possibly of sand or gravel paths. Water pipes tend to survive well in the soil, but it may not be possible to determine if they were for fountains or some other use. When medieval garden features have been removed, it soon becomes difficult to tell that they had ever existed, as I can vouch from experience.

Unfortunately, there are no medieval gardens that have survived intact, although the sites of the monastic and castle gardens are often known. The area of land that was once the vineyard at what is now Peterborough Cathedral is still known as such, but the chance of excavations finding the original garden layout are limited as the land has been built on. The smaller gardens in castle areas are often impossible to investigate as the areas within the curtain walls were remodelled over the years as castles changed in use from being primarily for defence and a statement of power to luxurious domestic dwellings. It is only in more recent times that archaeologists were even interested in gardens and the taking of soil samples to understand what may have been planted. Thankfully, there are some good sites that have survived rather well.

Tintagel

One small garden site has probably survived at Tintagel Castle. The garden is recorded by the antiquary and writer John Leland who visited Tintagel in 1540 during his six-year tour of England to record documents and the antiquities of the realm. He recorded the site as: 'A ground quadrant walled as yt were a garden plot.'

Archaeologists have little hard evidence, but general opinion is that it is reasonable to assume that this is a garden, and it could date from between the 1230s and the fifteenth century when it fell into ruin. The garden is situated about 130m beyond the

The remains of the garden at Tintagel Castle.

protection of the Inner Ward wall and is slightly protected from the westerly winds, as it is just below the highest point of the rising land. There is a spring about 45m to the northwest, which would be useful for a gardener. The remains are a rectangular enclosure of 20m by 14m, surrounded by a wall about 0.9m high and which varies in thickness from 1.2m to 1.5m. There is no indication of how high the walls would have been, but they may have been tall enough to protect anybody inside from the wind. The entrance, just under a metre wide, leads into the enclosure where a small border 0.5m wide runs around the base of the wall. A narrow path runs just inside the border and another divides the plot into two. Slates are set edgeways to mark the paths.

Whittington Castle

Another promising site of a medieval garden can be found in the Welsh Marches at Whittington Castle, near Oswestry. It was abandoned and may yet yield clues to layout, construction and possibly even some planting details. The castle is now a ruin surrounded by a moat. The site made the headlines when archaeologist Peter Brown announced that the site of the medieval garden had been discovered.

A geophysical survey appears to indicate paths and beds for plants with water being used to enhance the visual appearance of the castle, rather than for

Site of Whittington Castle garden.

defensive purposes. Evidence suggest that the garden was created between 1310 and 1330, possibly by Fulk VI, who had married Eleanor, sister of Sir John de Beauchamp of Hatch in Somerset. Eleanor seems to have been a strong woman who was more than capable of looking after the castle while her husband was away for his numerous military campaigns. Was Eleanor the person who had the garden made?

The major dispute about this garden is the mount. Mounts are a common garden feature of later formal gardens, but there are earlier mentions of mottes or mounds in gardens. In 1366 the mound at Dalton was mown and the chamberlain of Durham Priory notes that the hay was worth 3s 4d. Another reference to early mounds comes from Caxton in 1483 when he says that brambles and their berries are often found in gardens on mottes. There is no documentary evidence for the mound at Whittington being built. The original motte for the earlier castle is recorded as being encapsulated within the inner bailey that was built in the 1220s. Although mounts in gardens are usually said to be of a much later date, the mount at Whittington is aligned with the garden, which suggests that it may be contemporary with the garden, but not necessarily.

Artist's impression of how Whittington Castle garden may have appeared. (With kind permission of richardallenillustrator.com)

As yet there are no plausible alternative suggestions of why the mount is there. There is a possibility of foreign influence. Just before the Battle of Dupplin Moor against the Scots, Fulk rallied his troops, telling them that he had fought against the Saracens. The date is too late for him to have been on a crusade in the Holy Land, but he could have been fighting in Spain during the *Reconquista* to drive the Islamic settlers out of Spain. It is possible that Fulk had seen Islamic gardens and was inspired to create his own garden in the Welsh Marches. It is a wonderful idea, but until further research can be carried out, we must dream on.

Sycarth Castle

During the late fourteenth century, Owain Glyndŵr had a castle at Sycarth, not so far from Whittington Castle, of which the poet Iolo Goch sang its praises.

The moated castle was so luxurious that the dressing rooms are compared to the finest goods that were on sale at Cheapside in London. The towers were roofed with

The remains of Sycarth Castle.

slates. There was a lime-washed cross and the chapel had stained glass. Outside were an orchard and a vineyard. The dovecote is said to have shone, so it was probably painted with limewash. A constantly flowing stream powered a mill and probably fed into the sheltered fishponds which were well-stocked, ready for somebody to cast their nets to catch dinner. Rabbits, a high-status food, also providing a soft fur for clothing, were kept in a warren. And finally, to show off the status of the castle's owner, peacocks and cranes strutted in the grounds. It was, as the poet said, a fair place. Sadly, little remains, only grassy mounds because Owen's castle and gardens were razed to the ground by English soldiers during his rebellion.

Kenilworth Castle

One of the grandest gardens was at Kenilworth. Outside of the castle there was once a great lake called the mere, which King John enlarged to half a mile long and over 150 yards wide. The lake was partly defensive and partly practical as it provided water to drive two mills, but it was also decorative, providing a home for water birds and fish.

A GUIDE TO MEDIEVAL GARDENS

View over the site of Kenilworth Mere from the castle wall.

The *Pleasaunce*, a pleasure garden, was built in 1414 for Henry V, situated slightly north west of the castle on the edge of the Great Mere. Called by Henry *Le Pleasauntz en Marys*, the Pleasure Garden in the Marsh, the garden was designed as a place to escape from court life.

As with most pleasure gardens it was secluded and exclusive. Thomas Elmjam wrote a biography of Henry V, including his improvements at Kenilworth, reporting that the area had previously been a wild, wasteland of briars and thorns that was inhabited by foxes. The site was cleared and a timber framed banqueting house was built within a walled courtyard. Encircling moats were dug to ensure privacy.

Higham Ferrers Castle

Little remains of the castle now except for parts of the moat, an open space that was one of the wards and the partial remains of a dovecote and the land that was the upper ward. There was a small garden within the castle walls, as 31s 9d was spent on rebuilding a piece of stone wall between the steward's chamber and the small garden. This was quite a considerable amount of money, but it included the stone, the mortar, and the wages for the men digging out the stone. Higham Ferrers was a very important castle, being owned by many important families: the Peverels, de Ferrers, Lancasters and the king. Luckily, records have survived that give an insight on life at the castle and the sources of income that paid for a wealthy lifestyle. The local residents were probably typical of other large villages. They tended animals, grew and harvested crops and looked after the lord's park, fishponds and dovecotes. There were millers, butchers, bakers and dealers in linen. Some of the locals drank too much and some were keen on gambling. Women were tried as scolds and some men attacked others with daggers, but also with their agricultural and horticultural tools, including a shepherd's crook, a muck-fork, a pitchfork, a billhook and even a hurdle. Poachers killed deer, hares, rabbits, pheasants, partridges and plovers whilst fish were often stolen from the fishponds. One of the poachers was a priest who was caught hunting on a Sunday.

The castle site is thought to have been made up of three enclosures: the upper, lower and outer wards, although the latter two courts may have been merged. The lower ward had a garden with a pond slightly to the north of it. The garden was enclosed by a wall, but there are no clues as to what may have been grown there. Later the garden was rented out, so at this point the garden may have only been producing crops for sale. On the east ward side of the castle was a huge area called Bury Close where most of the functional buildings, the barns and stables were placed. There was also a conygree for breeding rabbits within the castle walls. Rabbits could be sold for 2d to 3d each, so selling the surplus was a good source of income. The castle possessed a vineyard that at one point covered at least three acres of land. There were other fishponds, three watermills that were valued at £8 per year, with a fishery at the mills worth 6s 8d per year and a windmill at Raunds which was worth 50s a year. The deer park is south east of the castle and about three miles away. To help stock the park, fifteen bucks and fifteen does were granted to William de Ferrers by the king in 1249. During the fifteenth century, there was a lodge for the park keeper to live in. The lodge had a hall, a chamber, a chapel, a bakehouse, a brewhouse and a kitchen. Close by there were two fishponds and a dovecote. The park keeper held the gate key to allow access to the park. The castle's income came from money paid as rent for housing and land, hens and eggs paid as rents, labour due, fines from courts and knight's fees. There was also a fine known as a merchet, which meant that if you were a bond tenant, your daughter could only marry outside the manor with the lord's permission and a fee. Adeline Richard had to pay 3s 4d when daughter Anastasia became married. The castle held the rights to the local market with an income from renting out the stalls, and the annual fair held at the festival of St Botolph. The market site is still used as a farmer's market.

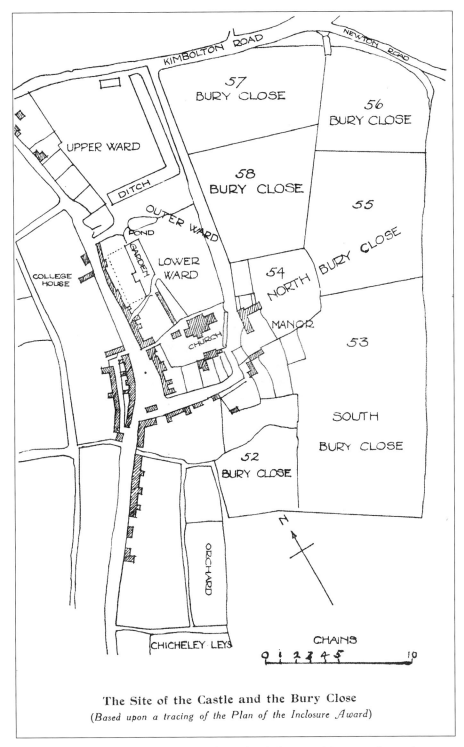

The Site of the Castle and the Bury Close
(*Based upon a tracing of the Plan of the Inclosure Award*)

Higham Ferrers Castle, showing a garden near the pond in the lower ward. (Courtesy of HiFars)

CHAPTER 2

Influences of European Medieval Gardens

Little is known of the English gardens in the Later Saxon period. Gardens specifically set aside for growing herbs were known from at the abbeys of Thorney and Ely in Cambridgeshire. The church and monastic system would have helped to preserve classical horticultural knowledge and techniques through the years following the collapse of the Roman Empire. The monks copied many classical books written by Roman authors such as Cato, Columella, Palladius and Varro that contained advice on choosing the best site for your house and gardens and how to run your estates for both profit and pleasure. There were instructions on how to tend to your animals, the growing of vines and grains and even recipes for the meals to feed your slaves. Knowledge could have been passed throughout the European monastic system by travelling clerics. Plants could also have been given as gifts, particularly those considered to have medicinal value.

The Norman Conquest had a major impact on the transformation of gardens in England. Many of William's military aristocracy had fought in Southern Italy and Sicily or been in contact with those that had. During the Crusades of 1095 to 1291, the tough northern knights passed through Byzantium and Arabia where they saw and would have been amazed by the opulence of eastern palace grounds. Within the carefully designed gardens was a lush growth of unknown exotic plants set against the extravagant use of water for pools with fountains and rills. Constantinople had been founded by the Roman Emperor Constantine in ad 330. This was the capital of the Eastern Roman empire until the city was captured by the Ottoman Turks in 1453. After Rome itself had fallen, Constantinople in the form of the Byzantine empire continued to safeguard the classical traditions and knowledge, proclaiming itself as the last remaining outpost of the Roman Empire. Charlemagne, the ruler of the Holy Roman Empire from Christmas Day ad 800, had been so impressed by the splendours of Constantinople that he had a copy made of the fountain from the garden of the Byzantine Emperor, making him one of the earliest members of the European upper classes to adopt foreign influences to establish decorative gardens as places to retire from the cares of the world and to impress visitors, and to indulge in a certain amount of one-upmanship too!

Agriculture and horticulture continued to be an important part of Byzantine life. A tenth century book, *Geoponika*, containing twenty chapters, continued the Roman tradition of estate manuals that instructed you on how to run your estates for profit and pleasure, with chapters ten to twelve mostly concentrated on horticulture. There were gardens to provide food, with orchards for fruit and nuts, vineyards and gardens for growing vegetables such as cabbages, carrots, courgettes, cucumbers, garlic, leeks, lettuce, melons and onions. For the wealthy, gardens were designed to give shade and to delight the senses. Trees were underplanted with crocus, iris, lilies, narcissus, periwinkle, roses and violets. Some of the shrubs and trees appear to have been pruned to enhance their beauty. There would be a plentiful supply of water flowing through a grid-system of channels. Pools contained fish to please the eye. Fountains added sound and cooled the air. Pots of plants were used to decorate roof gardens.

The Great Palace was created to impress. For over 800 years it was the official residence of the emperor, until Constantinople was sacked by the Christian soldiers of the fourth Crusade. The palace complex included many fine buildings, including residential areas, reception rooms, banqueting buildings, baths and chapels. For outdoor relaxation there were orchards, pleasure and vegetable gardens, fishponds, and areas for sports. One emperor took gardening to new levels. Constantine IX Monomachos was renowned for his megalomaniacal gardening feats. He would have meadows surrounded with fences. Soil would be carried in from forest groves. Whatever took his fancy, he would expect to have instantly. Trees and fruiting vines were transplanted by his gardeners on his whim. He expected nightingales and cicadas to move in equally quickly so they could fill his garden with their songs, or he became upset. Automata, machines driven by water, weights and pulleys, had continued in use from the Roman period. When Bishop Liudprand of Cremona visited the imperial palace at Constantinople in ad 968, he gave a detailed account of the royal throne, which was decorated with a gilded tree and singing birds. The wonders and marvels of the gardens of Constantinople and those of the Arabs must have filled the crusaders with amazement. Once they had returned home, the battle-weary crusaders possibly began to emulate what they had seen. Within castle grounds, turf seats, raised flowerbeds and fountains were built. Enclosed gardens, possibly used by courtly lovers, gave welcome privacy away from the bustle of the Great Hall.

In the secular world, rulers often travelled great distances to maintain their realms. It is likely that information would be exchanged between courts during their journeys. Travellers, including diplomats, merchants and pilgrims would bring back stories of wonders in other countries, which may have encouraged horticultural aspirations at home. Collecting seeds of flowers from the local plants to take home as souvenirs was most likely as common then as now.

CHAPTER 3

Monastic and Sacred Gardens

For Europeans during the middle ages, the Bible was the literal truth, with little leeway for open discussion. God had created the world and everything within it. God had made Adam, and later Eve, to be the custodians of the Garden of Eden, to carry out a minimal amount of toil to find their food and to maintain the garden. Natural rivers supplied the water, and all that Adam was required to do was, 'to dress it and to keep it'.

The Bible describes the Garden of Eden as a natural wilderness, with trees that would provide food, and which were pleasant to view. And all should have been well. But it was in this earthly paradise that the original sin took place. For regardless of the protective walls, evil was still able to enter the garden. Adam was prepared to live a life of simple pleasures, but Eve was tempted by the serpent to eat the forbidden fruit, and she in turn tempted Adam. Their disobedience caused God to expel them from their home, saying:

'Cursed is the ground for thy sake... thorns also and thistles shall it bring forth.
In the sweat of thy face shall you eat bread.'

And thus was mankind now cursed to endure the pains of hard labour to survive. Many medieval paintings depict Adam and Eve being thrown out of Eden through a defensive, but very stylish, gateway.

The church looked back to the Garden of Eden as a lost Golden Age to whence, with care and luck, we could return. More importantly for women, they came to be regarded as the cause of man's downfall and the objects of sin. It would take centuries of struggle for women to even begin to be recognised as equals.

The idea of Eden is mentioned in the *Glastonbury Chronicle* c.1350, where the author extolled the virtues of another earthly paradise, Glastonbury's island of apples, claiming that the fields were so fertile that no farmers were needed to tend them in order to produce a bountiful harvest of crops, apples and grapes.

Another source of biblical imagery for gardens was *The Song of Songs*, or *Solomon's Song*, a highly erotic and sensual poem that mixes sexual imagery with the symbolism of gardens and the plants that grew there. Solomon's beloved is safe within an enclosed garden:

Garden of Eden showing the temptation, expulsion and Adam and Eve toiling to earn their food. (Getty Image)

'A garden enclosed is my sister, my spouse,
A spring shut up; a fountain sealed.'

Symbolically the beloved is the garden itself. She is a virgin, protected from temptation, but also prevented from becoming a temptation to others through sealed seclusion. She hidden away from sight, effectively imprisoned within the garden. But it is a very beautiful prison. There are orchards of pomegranates, which with their many seeds are symbols of fertility. Mandrakes, said to be an aphrodisiac and bringers of fertility, grow there, and sweet flowers scent the air.

Although there is very little mention of the Virgin Mary in the Bible, the imagery of the *Song of Songs* would be taken into the growing cult of the Virgin Mary, and from there to the *Hortus Conclusus*, an enclosed or secret garden. The church presented Mary as the perfect woman, who had given birth and yet remained a virgin. In the enclosed abbeys, the unrelieved testosterone of the monks turned to the unattainable woman who was both perfect and pure: they chose a Heavenly passion.

The medieval poet John Lydgate must have been inspired by the *Song of Songs* when he wrote *A Balade in Commendation of Our Lady*, where he alludes to Mary as an enclosed garden that has no wicked weeds growing within it. She is a paradise garden that brings pleasure to the senses. She is a red rose without thorns and a fountain of clear flowing water.

The *Hortus Conclusus* hid within the protective patriarchal walls of either the monastery or a castle. This secretive garden was tiny compared to the extensive parks beyond the protective walls. It was introspective, but sometimes had views into the countryside beyond, whether through carefully contrived gaps in the hedges or by standing on the turf seats. The paintings of the time show the Virgin Mary, the flower of femininity, dressed as an aristocratic lady, the baby Jesus sitting on her lap or clasped to her breast. Mary is sitting within a summer garden in full bloom, the air fragrant with the heady scent of roses and lilies. Birds sing. The sky is a bright, clear blue. It never rains in medieval gardens! Mary is often accompanied by several female saints, also shown as high-status ladies, enjoying the pleasures that upper class ladies

of the time enjoyed in their gardens; namely, making roses circlets to wear on their head, reading and enjoying a time of leisurely relaxation, with apparently no cares in the world.

Mary symbolically became the garden, and many pictures show her within a walled garden, whilst the owner of the breviary is shown with the family knelt in prayer. Mary's, Immaculate Conception, literally from 'macula', meaning, without spot or stain, is suggested by her enclosure within the *Hortus Conclusus*.

The symbolism of Mary with a garden.
(Getty Image)

As in the Garden of Eden, there is usually a fountain of splashing water. The plants are beautiful, but nearly all are symbolic of Mary or Christ: white roses for purity for Mary and red roses for Christ and the blood of the martyrs, with lilies to show Mary's bodily purity and for the annunciation.

Iris flowers have three rising petals and three that fall, each set representing the trinity. The sharp, sword-like iris leaf represents the lance head thrust into Christ on the Cross. Violets are for Mary's innocence and humility and the sweet odours of heaven. The tri-lobed strawberry leaves reflect the Trinity, and the white flowers are for the bodily purity of Mary. The small red fruits represent the drops of blood from the Crown of Thorns. One story tells how Mary goes out with the souls of dead children to gather strawberries on mid-summer's morning. The garden is often the setting for scenes of the annunciation, when the archangel Gabriel tells Mary that she is going to give birth to Christ.

Annunciation. Mary in a wattle enclosed garden, c. 1400s. (Fitz-William Museum)

Garden Saints

There are surprisingly few gardening saints. Saint Fiacre, Fiachra or Fifrus, is thought to have come from Donegal in Ireland. He may have lived during the second part of the seventh century although the earliest written story of his life dates from the ninth century.

There are many variations of the story of how he left Ireland to arrive at Meaux, east of Paris, where he wanted to start a monastery. He asked Bishop Faor of Meaux for some land and was told he could have the land he turned over in a day with his spade. Most of us would have dug furiously to turn as much land as possible, but Fiacre was a wily Celt, so he dug a trench around the land that he wanted. He was probably a learned man as this is what the Romans did to mark out a new settlement. Other tales talk of assistance from angels, but another says they were not angels but

devils; or at least that is what a local woman, Becnaude, suspected when she told the bishop that she had seen with her own eyes devils helping Fiacre. The Bishop thought it best to withhold judgement until he had spoken with Fiacre himself. He decided in favour of Fiacre's version of what had happened, and thereafter, no woman would go into Fiacre's church for fear of becoming blind. St Fiacre is usually shown holding his metal-shod wooden spade. He was also the saint to pray to if you had piles! The abbey at Meaux still holds his relics. St Fiacre is celebrated on 11 August or 1 September.

Another garden saint is St Phocas, although his story is not so happy. He lived near the city of Sinope, now part of modern Turkey, close to the Black Sea, during the period

Saint Fiacre and Becnaude. (Getty Image)

of the Roman emperor Diocletian's persecution of Christians. Phocas was a hermit, spending his life in prayer and working in his garden, growing vegetables for the local poor; he also helped Christians to escape persecution. One day, two strangers came to his house and asked for lodging for the night. As was the custom, Phocas gave them food and a place to sleep. During the meal he asked their business in the area and they told him that they had been ordered to look for a Christian named Phocas, and to kill him. Later that evening, Phocas went outside and dug a grave in his garden, said his prayers and went to bed. The next morning, he gave the two men food and then told them that he was the man that they had been ordered to kill. The men were now reluctant to carry out their orders, but Phocas led them outside and showed them the grave that he had dug for himself. The men beheaded him and then buried his body in his own garden. St Phocas is celebrated on 23 February.

Dorothy was a woman who lived in what is now modern Turkey. She refused to give up her Christian faith, so was to be executed by beheading. Before her death she said that when she reached heaven, she would send an angel with fruit and flowers to prove that she had arrived there. Sure enough, the angel duly appeared with a basket of fruit and flowers, and as it was winter, this surely was a miracle! Saint Dorothy is usually shown with a basket of fruit and flowers. One picture shows her picking cherries in heaven, the fruit that the virtuous will be rewarded with once they arrive; truly an incentive to get to heaven. St Dorothy is celebrated on 6 February.

The monastic system began in the deserts of Egypt during the third and fourth centuries after the death of Christ. The monks escaped the world by going into the hot, sandy deserts to leave behind the temptations and troubles of the world. Initially, hermits went into the desert to live alone, but they attracted followers, and small communities developed rather haphazardly. The earliest monastic rule was written by St Pachomius, ad 292–348, who

St Dorothy. (Wellcome Collection)

established a monastery in Egypt on the island of Tebenna, in the River Nile. The ideas of Pachomius would set the tone for the way that monasticism would continue to develop. A description of Pachomius' community tells how the monks carried out many arts and crafts. There is mention of a man who worked in the garden and another who looked after the vegetable plot from which vegetables were picked for the monks' meals.

Unable to escape to sandy deserts, European monks fled to the wilderness of the many wild and uncultivated forests. The monks had to be self-sufficient. Over time they tamed and cleared the wilderness to create orchards, fishponds, dovecotes, vegetable gardens and fields for grains and animals. There would be gardens for meditation, to refresh the spirits and to remind them of a purer time in Eden. In the tenth century, the Irish monk, Manchán of Liath, built himself a cell, a chapel and a small garden to grow his vegetables. To supply his needs he kept hens, caught the speckled salmon, tended his bees for honey and wax and grew fresh, fragrant leeks.

The monks of Ely wrote of their refuge from the world with glowing praise:

'This island's dower is rich: fish, springs and ponds abound;
No stream flows but with fish... fertile land yields to the plough,
than which none richer may be found, nor readier to respond,
... All verdant grow the flow'ry meads: while blossom blows,
There's laughter in the grass. There, gardens numberless
Receive their dew from fountains, while a scent of flowers
Breathes forth – perpetual flowers that everywhere feign Spring,
Variously coloured, pleasing in diversity. There thickets proffer diverse fruit;
There apple-trees load branches down with heaviness;
There, equally, are pears and plums, delightful all.
Here, too, abundant honey flows from hives of bees:
This same Isle which bears honey pours forth milk in streams.'

This was, in reality, a land of milk and honey.

Maybe the monks' ideas of transforming the wilderness and waste lands were partly inspired by the bible:

'For the Lord shall comfort Zion: he will comfort all her waste places; and he will make her wilderness like Eden, and her desert like the garden of the Lord; joy and gladness shall be found therein, thanksgiving, and the voice of melody'.
Isiah 51 3

'You shall eat the fruit of the labour of your hands; you shall be happy, and it shall be well with you'.
Psalm 128.2

And there was even some gardening advice:

> 'For the land, whither thou goest in to possess it, is not as the land of Egypt, from whence ye came out, where thou sowest thy seed, and watered it with thy foot, as a garden of herbs.'
>
> *Deut. 11. 10*

Which suggests that there were channels of water which were opened to irrigate the plants with a deft kick of the foot.

The bible even described the life of an individual in terms of a garden:

> 'And the Lord shall guide thee continually, and satisfy thy soul in drought, and make fat thy bones: and thou shalt be like a watered garden, and like a spring of water, whose waters fail not.'
>
> *Isiah 58. 11*

St Benedict founded a monastery at Monte Cassino in Italy in ad 540. He also realised that a community needed rules so that the monks could live peacefully. The Rule of St Benedict was the system that most western monks would follow, although new orders were set up to reform the monastic system over the centuries. In Britain the Celtic monks lived as individuals with their own calculation for the date of Easter Sunday and a different tonsure (hair style) to the monks who followed the rule of Rome. The dates for Easter could be up to four weeks apart, which was not helpful for Christian unity. King Oswiu of Northumbria called both sides to a meeting at Whitby in 664 ce. After much discussion, Oswiu decided that he favoured the Roman clerics and their traditions.

The ethos for the Benedictine monks was made up of three activities: prayer, study and work. The monks gave prayer and devotion to the glory of God, to ensure their own personal salvation and that of others. They studied the Bible and other devotional works to help them have a better understanding, to make sure that doctrine was consistent and adhered to and to erase copying errors which it was difficult to avoid when manuscripts were copied by hand. Work itself could include copying manuscripts, carrying out craft activities such as metal work, leatherwork and pottery and tending the animals, fields and gardens, although Lay Brothers would often carry out the more laborious tasks. As time passed, the small communities became larger, requiring more land and buildings to run efficiently, and thus, more planning when a new monastery was established.

There is a plan made of five pieces of parchment sewn together that dates to the early 800s, from a monastery in Switzerland, which is usually known as the Saint

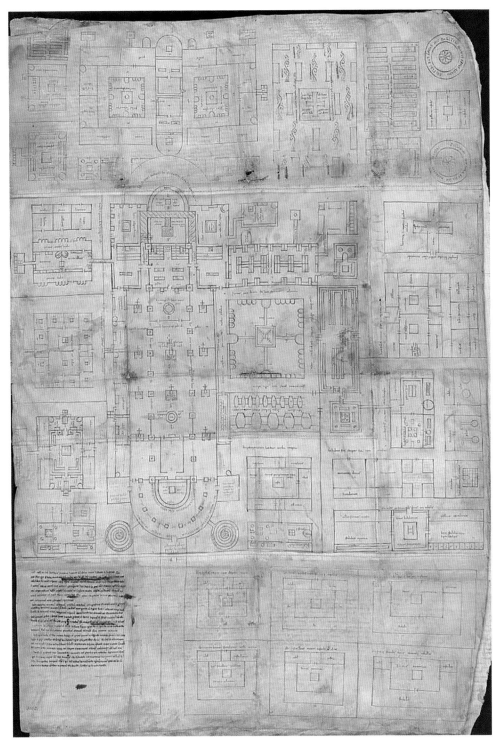

St Gall plan showing the layout of an ideal monastery. (Wiki Commons)

Gall plan. It shows the layout of the ideal monastery, incorporating everything a monastery would need to run effectively. There are workshops for saddlers, shoemakers, goldsmiths, smiths, turners, fullers and cutlers, with rooms for them to live in. There are stables for horses and oxen. Sheds for cows, pigs, goats and sheep. To provide sustenance there are kitchens, bakehouses and brewhouses. For education, there is a school, and fairly close by, a scriptorium and library. There are lodgings for distinguished guests, which are not far from the abbot's house, but to avoid having to mix with the lower classes, the lodgings for the poor guests are some distance away.

The church itself has a semi-circular paradise as you approach the common entrance and another paradise beyond the far walls. These paradises could possibly have been gardens, but not always, because the paradise at Santiago de Compostela in Northern Spain was described as being paved with stone.

A monastic settlement would need to grow plants for food, to decorate the church on festive occasions, to supply flavourings for drinks and for strewing herbs to scent many of the rooms.

The monks would also need to have a physic garden to provide the drugs needed to treat the sick, so there is a medicinal physic garden next to the doctor's house. The doctor was not only reliant on plant cures, and there was also a building for bloodletting. The plants in the physic garden are neither exotic nor particularly dangerous: there are beans, cumin, fennel, fenugreek, horsemint, iris, lily, lovage, mint, pennyroyal, rosemary, roses, rue, sage, savoury, and tansy.

The gardener's house overlooks the vegetable garden, which has the vegetables growing in rectangular beds. In reality there are not enough beds to provide the quantity of vegetables to feed a large monastic community; many of the vegetables would have been grown in the fields and the list is unlikely to include everything that was being grown. Fow example, peas are not included. The vegetables are shown as: beets, cabbages, carrots, celery, chervil, coriander, dill, garlic, gith (*nigella sativa*, a spice, sometimes sold as onion seed to flavour food), leeks, lettuce, onions, parsley, parsnip, poppy, radish, shallots and winter savoury. The vegetable garden is conveniently sited next to the poultry and duck pens, so that the birds can be easily fed with garden waste and pests such as caterpillars and slugs. The gardener's house was probably for the person who supervised the garden work as there are rooms for his servants besides storage rooms for tools and seeds.

Another important garden area is the orchard, which in this case also serves as a cemetery. The idea of a green burial ground has a longer history than most people realise. The St Gall plan shows one tree of each type in the orchard, but in reality, there would have been several rows of each tree. Another anomaly is that some of the trees, the fig and peach trees, are unlikely to have borne fruit, even if they had survived the climate. Whoever drew the plan was probably referring to classical authors, possibly one of the estate manuals, as inspiration for the plants that could be grown. Medieval man was eminently practical and would use features for more than one purpose if possible. The orchard cemetery symbolically reflects the idea that mankind originally came from the Garden of Eden and would return to a physical and paradisiacal garden upon death. The exquisite painting, *The Little Garden of Paradise*, by Städel, c. early 1400s, probably as an altarpiece, measures only 26.3 x 33.4cm. The detail is so good that individual plants and birds are easily recognised. Mary, deeply engrossed in her book, is seated next to a table on which there is food and drink. St Dorothy picks cherries from a tree that has two trunks entwined together. A female saint ladles a drink of water from a shallow well. The baby Jesus plucks a psaltery, and a baby dragon lays on its back, as if waiting for somebody to tickle its tummy.

Heaven could be imagined as a garden. (Wiki Commons)

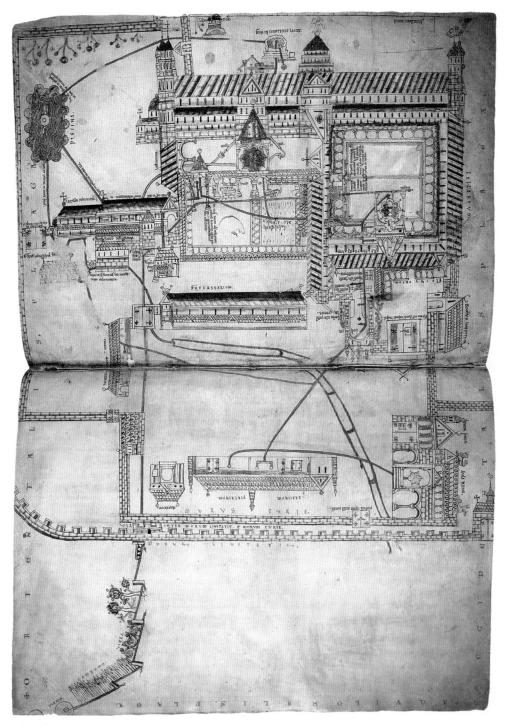

Plan of Prior Wibert's water system. (Wiki Commons)

A similar plan to that of St Gall has survived in England. Shown is a plan of the water works implemented by Prior Wibert at Christchurch, Canterbury, dating to around 1165. It shows the water flowing through cornfields, orchards and vineyards as it approaches the boundary walls. Having entered the precinct, the water is led to an elaborately shaped *piscina*, a pool for fish, and from there to the storage tower, from where it is redirected around the rest of the site. The water tower can still be seen today.

The Water Tower, Canterbury.

As in the St Gall document, the plan shows a garden cemetery, with the plants all drawn upside-down. This could have been an orchard or garden for contemplation on the brevity of life. A *herbarium*, a small garden, in this case cloistered, is shown but there are no details of the plants growing in it. The garden is close to the infirmary, so it may have been used as a pleasant place for recovering monks to enjoy the fresh air, for growing medicinal plants, or it was possibly a combination of both. The great cloister of a monastery is an open square space, enclosed by covered walkways that were often lavishly decorated. Many cloisters had paths crossing from the sides, that could symbolise the crucifixion. In Britain the cloister is usually placed on the south side of the church for maximum sunlight and warmth. The open space seems to have commonly been planted with grass, as green was regarded as a colour that would aid meditation and reflection. The monk William of Auvergne suggested that green was a soothing colour as it was the mid-point between black and white. Bright light causes the pupil of the eye to close and the darkness of black causes the pupil to open, so green was the ideal colour for resting the eyes. It is possible that one or two evergreens, such as yew, were grown in the cloister to represent eternal life. In many cloisters there would often be a source of water, and a covered well can still be seen at Peterborough Cathedral. The semi-circular Paradises shown on the St Gall church may have been gardens and cemeteries, with the eastern end reserved for the higher status clergy who would want to be buried as close to the high altar as possible. At the east end of Peterborough cathedral, medieval graves we uncovered and moved. Several of the stone coffins were dug up, and can now be seen arranged near the chancel wall. The abbot would usually have his own private garden. In 1302, Abbot Godfrey of Crowland spent the huge sum of £25 to build a large garden at Peterborough Abbey next to the Derby Yard. It was surrounded by double moats and trees were planted. These gardens overlooked the banks of the River Nene and were little changed when the map-maker Speed visited Peterborough sometime around 1651. The site of the garden has now been lost to development.

The most important monastic garden was the responsibility of the cellarer, who ensured that the monks would be properly fed. The garden would provide the vegetables, herbs, peas, beans, leeks, onions and garlic that were the basic ingredients for the pottage that the monks ate on most days. This important position required a man with a good business sense and a knowledge of plants. He had to be capable of careful planning to ensure that the food supply would not run out. The cellarer was responsible for selling surplus produce from the gardens and orchards and for buying in extra food if the crops had failed in any particular year. He was also responsible for buying things that couldn't be produced in his own gardens. At Battle Abbey, successive cellarers bought almonds, figs, ginger, galingale and zeodary (both have roots that are used in a similar way to ginger), white peas for pottage and sacks of expensive saffron. So much for the monks having a sparse life!

In 1332, Simon Crump, the cellarer of Worcester was granted the aid of a clerk to help him fulfil his duties for the rest of his life. Simon had risked his life at land and sea, travelling to Rome for the benefit of Worcester, and this was his reward. His new assistant, Robert de Wornesleye, was to be given a loaf of bread per day, one flagon of the best beer, and on both flesh and fish days he was to have pottage and any other dishes that were customarily given to one of the monks' helpers. He would also receive the same type of clerical gown as the cellarer's accountant every year, which suggests that some cellarers had several people to supervise and probably did not do much of the practical gardening themselves.

The Infirmary Garden provided the herbs used to make medicines for those within the community and probably outside too. Herbs were an important part of early medicine; growing your own meant that you knew just how the plants had been grown, which was important when gauging their potency. You would also be certain the plants were what they were claimed to be, as some common herbs are even now mistaken for poisonous ones that are similar in appearance. Mandrake and opium poppies, although poisonous, could be grown for their painkilling properties. There was a medical theory that the body had four liquids in it: blood, black bile, yellow bile and phlegm. If the liquids became too much out of balance, you would become ill. Blood could soon be brought back into balance by cutting a vein. To bring the other three humours back into balance you could be purged. This would be by using plants to induce vomiting, diarrhoea and sweating which would bring the four liquid humours of the body back into balance and thus make you well again. There were several plants that were used to remove intestinal worms and many others for the bite of mad dogs and venomous insects.

The Sacristan would need a garden to provide flowers for decorating shrines, altars and large candles, and to celebrate the many feast days during the liturgical year. The Catholic church celebrates many events that occurred during the life of the Virgin Mary, so flowers symbolic of Mary would be needed for every season to decorate the church, especially lilies and other white or sweet-scented blossoms. On feasts days it was customary for flowers to be made into circlets, being worn like crowns on the head, an idea dating back to the Romans which continued in use for centuries after. The priests of St Mary Hill, London, wore garlands of roses and other flowers for the celebrations of Corpus Christi and St Barnabus.

Another expense for the Sacrist was the church service for the singing of the psalm that was known as *O of the Gardener*, from the third of the seven Gregorian great Psalms that begin with 'O'. In this case it is the psalm beginning 'O *Radix Jesse*,' which would be sung by the *hortulanus*, the priest in charge of the gardens.

The Benedictine monks may have led a communal life, but the Carthusian order, founded in 1084, was an eremitical order, meaning that each monk would effectively be living as a hermit, spending most of his life alone in his cell, only leaving to join the communal services in the church. Each monk had his own individual cell with its own garden. The monk was allowed to have pens, ink and other materials for writing and the tools he would need to carry out a trade to earn money. He could tend his garden in whatever way he wished.

The best place so see a Carthusian monastery in Britain is Mount Grace Priory in North Yorkshire, where one of the cells and its garden have been restored. There was even a channel of water to flush the toilet clean. A few of the gardens were excavated by archaeologists in the 1980s. The layout of one of the early sixteenth century cell-gardens showed that it had three rectangular beds that were edged with stones and that one of the beds had a circular arrangement of stones within it. Flowerpots were discovered in another garden and there were indications of planting holes for trees or shrubs. The majority of the gardens have yet to be examined, so maybe a later excavation will reveal more details of the manner in which different monks made use of their gardens.

When considering monasteries, it is easy to forget that many religious houses were for women. There has not been as much research on how nuns ran their establishments, but records survive showing that their estates were run much the same as those of the monks, but to protect them from unwanted male attention, extra security and restrictions were desirable, if not always effective.

One of the earliest references to the nuns having decorative gardens comes from a story about King Rufus. Matilda, who would later become the wife of Henry I, was

A recreation of a garden for a monk's cell at Mount Grace Priory.

receiving an education from the nuns at the convent of Romsey under the protection of her aunt, Christina, who was the abbess. One day, when Matilda was twelve, King Rufus and some of his knights demanded entrance to the grounds. Christina feared for the girl's safety and made her wear a nun's veil. The king was allowed to enter, his excuse being that he wished to admire the roses and other flowers that grew in the garden. The abbess had arranged that the nuns should walk through the garden, so that the king would see Matilda dressed as a nun. Once he had seen the veiled Matilda, Rufus made his excuses and left.

The Cellaress of a convent had the same tasks as that of her male counterpart, needing to ensure that food was readily available and paying the wages of hired labourers. At St Radegund's, Cambridge, the nuns employed John Speed to work in the gardens and other help was hired in to prune and tie the vines and to prune trees and chop firewood. They also employed the indomitable, multi-tasking Katherine Rolf, first mentioned in the accounts of 1449–50, when she was employed for four days to weed the garden for 4½d. Later she was paid 1½d a day for twelve days for her help with thatching two buildings. The following year she was assisting the candle-makers to make 14 lb of tallow candles. Afterwards she was paid to comb and clean a pound of wool ready for spinning and then she worked in the granary threshing and winnowing grain for the maltster. In the meantime, she appears to have been breeding chickens too, because she was also selling fat chickens to the nuns.

Convents aimed to be self-sufficient as much as possible. In 1319, the nuns of the Cistercian convent of St Mary at Syningthwaite in West Yorkshire were ordered to employ a proficient gardener to ensure a good supply of vegetables. There are very few manuscript pictures of nuns enjoying their gardens, but with few other pleasures in life the garden must have played an important part in their lives. In 1311 Bishop Woodlock ordered that: 'There shall be an entrance into the garden by a gate or postern for the sick for their recreation and solace.' Similarly, in 1310, it was recorded at Clementhorpe that a nun who was confined to the cloister for penance was allowed: 'for recreation and solace, to go into the orchard and gardens of the nunnery accompanied by nuns'. Some nuns appear to have preferred their garden to their religious duties. It was noted in 1440 that the nuns of Nuncotham, Lincolnshire, had their own private gardens, and that some of them did not attend the service of Compline. Instead, they walked in their gardens, picking herbs. With centuries of being self-sufficient and copying classical texts, religious establishments had acquired the knowledge and practical experience to develop horticulture through the early medieval period that used to be known as the Dark Ages. As European civilisation became more settled, they were able to disseminate their expertise to the wider community.

CHAPTER 4

Secular Gardens

Secular pleasure gardens were created for enjoying sensual delights. On warm, summer days you could escape the busy, noisy confines of the hall to the more intimate private gardens. There you were able to enjoy blue skies and soothing sunshine, with the drowsy humming of insects and softly cooing doves. Hot thirsty birds sip the cool refreshing water of the bubbling, splashing fountain and the heady scent of roses and lilies wafts on the warm air. The ladies could make chaplets of roses and talk or sing of love and maybe dance as they relaxed in the garden. These are the pleasure gardens that were lauded in medieval poetry and song and shown in lavishly illustrated manuscripts.

Religious and secular gardens were physically identical, with the same features of sweet-scented herbs, trees for shade, turf seats, rose-covered arbours, and flowery turf; there were important differences but these are mental concepts. It is not the physical garden that has changed but the perception of the lady within it. Is she human or is she divine?

In the secular world, this was a time when marriage was undertaken for financial gain, political bargaining and the strengthening of family ties. Children of a very young age would be betrothed as a part of political settlements. Love did not often come into the equation.

A leather reliquary showing Mary in a garden with the baby Jesus, but Romantic Love would replace her with a more worldly lady. (National Leather Collection, Northampton)

Andreas Capellanus wrote a treatise, *The Art of Courtly Love,* for Eleanor of Aquitaine, stating quite bluntly that one of the Laws of Love, was that love could not exist between a man and his wife. Courtly Love, *Fin Amour,* was exclusive, not inclusive. It was strictly for the powerful, young, wealthy, healthy and beautiful. Secular gardens became the setting for quests in search of love and physical satisfaction, so we have moved from a garden that preserves the integrity of the Lady, to a garden where that integrity is purposefully challenged. This is now the very *raison d'être* of the Garden of Love.

The physical features in sacred and secular gardens were identical. It is the symbolism behind them that was different.

The twelfth century poems and songs tend to be set, not in gardens, but in the surrounding countryside with flowery meadows and trees for shade and privacy. The *pastourelles* usually tell of a knight seducing a shepherdess. Sometimes the singer is the woman, as in the German Minnesinger song, *Under der Linden,* where, following the inevitable seduction under a lime tree, the woman reflects that:'If anybody knew that he lay with me, I am ruined, Tandaradei!'

Sometimes the poems move into an orchard, where maybe there will be a clear fountain, and roses and nightingales make frequent appearances. The woman is a flower of beauty, with lily white skin and rose cheeks.

Boccaccio set his book, the *Decameron,* within a garden. It was a refuge for the lords and ladies to escape the dangers of the plague ravaging the countryside. The garden has hints of biblical themes. There are walls and a gate to keep out the plague-ridden populace, but once inside there is the central fountain that provides the living waters to everything that grows within the garden, echoing the four rivers of paradise. The trees give shade but are delightful to see, and produce fruit, reminding us of the forests of Eden. There are animals of about a hundred kinds that run around, as if tame. The rich storytellers think themselves in a new Eden, safe from the plague, but of course, as with the original Eden, it cannot last forever. It is another illusion set in a garden, as many other dreams and illusions were.

Although medieval poetry and song often placed its themes within a garden, it is also a common device that the poet finds himself within a dream. The most famous dream garden was that in the *Roman de la Rose.* The poem is set in the month of May, which in Europe is the time of new beginnings and possibilities. Birds sing, flowers blossom and the thoughts of nature and man turn to procreation and love. In the Garden of Love, it is eternally the month of May. The garden is entered by a locked gate, the keys being held by Lady Idleness, who vets those wishing to gain entry. There will be no poverty in this garden. Ideally there should be no covetousness, envy nor hatred, and in the earlier original version by the French poet Lorris in the early thirteenth century, there wasn't. But when de Meun decided to complete the poem nearly fifty years later, they were added with a vengeance. Violence enters the paradise, and the rose is won by physical assault, rather than *Amour Courtoise*, Courtly Love. On entering the garden, the poet remarks that the garden is as long as it is wide, with the corners set at right angles. The formal layout of the garden as a nearly perfect square, is possibly a reference to St John's description in Revelations, of the four-square city, although some artists illustrating copies of the *Roman de la Rose* completely ignored references to the square and painted the enclosing walls as being circular. Within the garden walls are evenly spaced exotic trees, such as grains of paradise and date palms. This may be poetic licence, but it is possible that wealthy owners in warmer climates could have grown plants that others did not have at the time. Gardeners always try to grow exotic plants, regardless of the chances of long-term success and such exotic plants may have survived in some gardens until killed by harsh unseasonal weather. For the lovers there is turf as soft as a feather bed. This is a garden designed to tempt the visitors into sensuous, languid idleness. The fountains and streams are crystal clear, without the slimy newts, the frogs that noisily croak, nor the stench of stagnant waters that plagued most of the fountains and pools throughout early European garden history. But the secret of this fountain is powerful. It is adorned with magic crystals and silver gravel to attract the eye; and then the gazer is captured and doomed, because this is the fountain of Narcissus.

The Pearl is another poem set within a dream, concerning a different type of love, but one that is equally transient. The setting is much the same as any other medieval poetical garden. The man is driven by love, but this time it is the story of a father's search for his dead daughter, the pearl of his dream. The garden transforms, but spiritually, rather than just physically, as is the case for the *Roman de la Rose*. The father is given a glimpse of his daughter in heaven but is then promptly returned to his normal mortal state, where he bemoans his fate.

One animal frequently shown in medieval art is the mythical unicorn. The unicorn was often symbolic of Christ. He was pure and innocent, and on occasion, violent, as was Christ himself when he threw the money lenders out of the temple. The unicorn inhabited the flowery meads and the enclosed gardens and parks of the millefleurs tapestries.

Medieval Bestiaries, which described real and fantastical creatures, told how the horn of a unicorn dipped into a poisonous liquid would render the poison harmless. The horn of a unicorn was of huge value to those who feared being removed from power by poisoning. Hunting unicorns was considered to be extremely dangerous, until the hunters discovered that the unicorn could be lured with a virgin, who represents the Virgin Mary.

Trusting in the maiden's purity, the unicorn would lay his head on her lap, and at that point the hunter could safely kill it and remove its horn. Symbolically this is a reenactment of the crucifixion. The cruelties of the world have finally broken through the protective boundaries of the *Hortus Conclusus*.

A unicorn in a flowery mead. (Wiki Commons)

The much-loved stories of Romantic literature may have encouraged people to create their own gardens, inspired by the ones that they imagined. This isn't an entirely fanciful idea because there are many records of knights fighting in tournaments that were based on a theme inspired by myths and legends, such as those about King Arthur. The knights and ladies would dress to suit the theme and pretend to be the individual characters of a particular tale, so in a similar fashion, gardens could easily have been created to reflect the ideals of Courtly Love and other romantic literature.

A GUIDE TO MEDIEVAL GARDENS

CHAPTER 5

Medieval Garden Features

The Pleasure Garden

Medieval gardens were not so different to our modern gardens and many features we use today were known in medieval gardens. Albertus Magnus described in detail the appearance of a typical medieval garden that was designed purely for pleasure. There should be lawn, surrounded by flower beds; this type of garden is common even today. The garden at Tintagel Castle is similar to the ideal that Albertus describes. There is a narrow stone-edged flowerbed that runs around the inside of the garden, enclosing the lawns.

Narrow flower bed at the base of the garden wall at Tintagel.

There should be trees for shade, but not placed too closely together, nor too close to the paths, or spider webs would catch the faces of passers-by! There should be a fountain or basin of water. The plants were to be sweetly scented, with a bench for people to sit and admire the delights surrounding them. Albertus stresses that these plants are for pleasure, they were not to be harvested for practical use, so although the plants are those that have many practical uses, there would be no trimming of the rosemary to flavour food, nor removing the rose petals for distillation. The plants are to be grown purely for the delight of their colours, scent and texture alone. For more contemporary advice on gardens, we can turn to a fourteenth century Italian lawyer, Pietro de Crescenzi. His book, *Ruralium Commodorum*, was published in 1346. Crescenzi followed the medieval tradition of taking his ideas from any source available to him and rewriting it as his own work but giving it authority by quoting acknowledged experts from the past. He based his book on the previously mentioned Roman estate manuals, with additional material from Pliny. Showing lack of bias, Crescenzi included information from Avicenna, the Arabian medical author, when he is presenting the medicinal uses of the plants that he suggests should be grown. It is unlikely that Crescenzi foresaw just how popular his book would become, as it has been translated into many languages from the original Latin, but as far as we can tell, it was never translated into English; certainly, no such copy exists. This would not be a problem for the clergy who could read Latin, nor the upper social circles, who prided themselves on speaking French, if they wanted to follow his advice. Crescenzi starts with the basics. The house should be sited in a sheltered place with a plentiful supply of water. To harvest good crops, you require a good fertile soil. You also need woodland to provide building materials and fuel. He dedicates his twelve chapters to the work needed to maintain and improve woodland, fields and vineyards. He describes the uses of the plants and how to grow and harvest them. As Crescenzi was writing in Italy, there is a large section on growing the grape vine and winemaking. Another chapter is dedicated to buying livestock and then keeping your animals in good health. Hunting for birds and animals was another method of providing food, so we are given instructions for hunting with hawk and hound, for fishing and how to make various traps. To ensure that you can instruct your labourers correctly throughout the year, the final chapter is a calendar that sets out the labours of the months.

At last we have an author writing about what he sees in contemporary gardens, even if he is basing some of his ideas on the wisdom of the past. Unfortunately, we cannot be sure that this is what is happening in British gardens of the time. Yet Britain was not an isolated backwater of Europe. The English were spending considerable time in France, fighting the Hundred Years' War. Merchants were crossing the known world in search of goods, and the clergy were communicating with foreign monasteries. The upper classes in Britain were not going to be left behind by their European contemporaries if they could help it; later in the Tudor period, King Henry VIII owned a copy that is still in the Royal collection.

Crescenzi copied the description of a medieval garden by Albertus Magnus but added information of his own, including information about a park-like garden as well as smaller decorative gardens. He said that the size of your garden should reflect your social standing. An emperor or king could have a park-type garden of twenty jugers or more; a juger being as much land as you could plough in a day and thus the size can vary, depending on the type of soil in your area. It would be approximately an acre. There should be trees for shade planted twenty feet apart so that each tree had plenty of space to grow to its natural extent. Close by you should plant sweet smelling herbs such as basil, sage, hyssop, feverfew and mint. You should also grow plants with attractive flowers, such as roses, violets and lilies.

Gardens of this large size were obviously positioned outside the castle or monastic walls, but within the walls smaller garden areas were placed in convenient spots, often aligned to the private rooms of individuals. This is noticeable at Rockingham Castle, Northamptonshire, where an area near the drum towers is still known as Queen Eleanor's Garden. Records show that Edward I had a chamber and door built for the Queen's corridor and that the nearby *viridarium*, a garden of grass, possibly with trees for shade, was enclosed by walls:

‘to Michael de Welydon, John de Cottingham and Maurice de Stanerne, layers making walls about the viridarium near the Chamber of the Queen, 3s 6d.’

This would give the Queen a place for privacy within the castle grounds and a view into her garden. It may have only been possible to enter the garden from her room. Remarkably, the site is still a garden of sorts, although no archaeological work has

The site of Queen Eleanor's garden at Rockingham Castle.

Medieval courtyard garden, Rye Castle.

A GUIDE TO MEDIEVAL GARDENS

been carried out to determine whether or not traces of Eleanor's garden have survived beneath the turf.

A small courtyard garden has been created at Rye Castle that demonstrates how many medieval garden features can be fitted into a small space.

Where the garden was not directly beneath your rooms, another way to ensure privacy and restrict access to your pleasure garden was to have a stout door which could be locked. Locked doors are shown in many manuscripts and in Chaucer's *Merchants Tale*, the elderly husband, Old January, keeps the key to the garden on his person, jealous that his younger wife may meet a lover there. In this he failed, as she was able to take the key and have a copy made.

Topiary

Very little structure is shown in the pictures of the small medieval gardens. They seem to have be created for use in the spring and summer months. Except for some fencing and the occasional topiarised shrub, most of the garden would have been flat in the winter months once the plants had died down. Topiary gives vertical impact to a garden. The Romans had made great use of topiary, clipping trees and shrubs into many different shapes, including people, animals, buildings and ships.

By the medieval period the practice appears to have died out. There are neither written nor pictorial records of the complicated shaping of trees and bushes until the fourteenth century, when topiary seems to have had a revival, but it would not reach its previous status again until the Renaissance. The medieval form of topiary, from our limited evidence, was cut to appear like a tiered wedding cake of no more than three layers. Were the three layers perhaps symbolic of the Holy Trinity? Sometimes, the top portion is domed, but mostly the illustrations show it as being flat.

This form was used for topiary in plain and decorative flowerpots, larger plants in flower beds and for tall trees where the cut-work starts at around head height. The topiary form is usually known as an estrade. Many of these trained plants are shown with a wooden wheel-like structure onto which the plants are trained. There is no need for a frame to be used in order to train plants in this way, as it is a simple matter to cut and shape them freehand.

Frames are also shown supporting other flowers. In one illustration the wood has been painted to look like jewels on a crown-like frame. Maybe the frame for the topiary gave a good visual effect whilst the plant was being trained. In some cases, it is possible that the branches had been grafted together to form a circular outer edge. Removing a small amount of bark on both stems and tying them together would be enough to achieve this, or a different graft could be used. One painting

Small estrade in a pot.

Medieval topiary, Prebendal Manor.

clearly shows the outer rim of the circular support, which appears similar to a bicycle wheel, with marks where the spokes fit. This suggests that the rim was made of a split stem. This may be possible with elder, that is then steamed to bend it into a circle.

Turf Seats

These are the most popular garden feature of all, if the illuminated manuscripts are a true reflection of real life, and is the major feature of the *Hortus Conclusus*, where Mary is often shown in a garden.

Albertus Magnus said that you should have a bench in the garden. If the illustrations are to be believed this was a turf seat. Wooden benches, portable or otherwise are not shown in the paintings of the period. The shape and position of the seats varied. Some seats are shown against a wall, others are independent and shown in small, enclosed gardens or in larger spaces with trees growing around them.

The simplest form of the turf seat is like a raised rectangular flower bed, but there are seats with three sides, like a large U. One English picture shows a hexagon with one side omitted, whilst a French picture shows a seat with separate brick-lined enclosure for individual couples, with musicians standing on the raised turf seat and dancers below them.

At its simplest the seat could be constructed entirely faced with turf, as shown in the *Luttrel Psalter*, although this appears to be the only sunken turf seat depicted in art. What is not believable are the perfectly vertical turf sides shown in some paintings. If the sides are perfectly vertical the turf soon dies. Having made a similar type of seat, the only way that I could keep the grass alive was by making sloping sides. The seat survived for several years with little maintenance, other than clipping the grass, until destroyed by children playing on it.

Later turf seats are shown faced with wooden planks, brick stone and wattle fencing. The verticals of the wattle are shown extending for some distance beyond the top of the seat, so maybe they were not that comfortable, or there was a certain

Ladies making circlets on a turf seat.

amount of artistic license. A simple turf seat can stand alone, but most turf seats are shown backed with trellis fencing over which the red and white roses have been carefully trained. If the turf seat forms part of an enclosure, the scent from the roses will be trapped within the turf seat area, making it a very sensual place to enjoy your leisure time. If you wished to retreat from the hustle and bustle of a busy hall, where better to go than an enclosed garden with a turf seat, where you could be served food and drink at a trestle table, with a minstrel to entertain you with songs of love and heroic, chivalrous deeds.

Tree Seat

Tree seats were designed to give shade. They were a turf seat with a tree growing out from the seat itself. Tree seats were quite varied in construction, often with the tree trimmed into three layers, like the estrade topiary form. Those in rural

settings are often shown with wattle sides. They were most likely intended for use by travellers or for labourers to rest or eat in a place out of the heat of the sun. Tree seats are also shown in gardens; the base is of wattle, brick, wooden planks or in some instances, finely carved stone, as in the painting *The Martyrdom of St Sebastian* in the British Library, where Sebastian has been tied to a tree within a courtyard and has been shot by archers.

Martyrdom of St Sebastian.
(Getty Image)

Tree Arbour

There is another form of seating that is shown in the background of a painting, *The Mystical Marriage of Saint Catherine*, from c.1490. The foreground shows the familiar Virgin on a turf seat within the *Hortus Conclusus*, but in the background two ladies sit in the shade of trees grown side by side like a hedge, which has been cut back to the trunks to form a shady arbour.

Tree arbour.

At the Prebendal Manor, a similar tree arbour was made using a mature hawthorn tree that overlooked the fishponds. It was a simple task to cut the outside into a neat dome and then cut into one side to create enough space to add a small stone seat. The result was a small arbour with pleasant views over the ponds and the fields beyond. The space within needed little maintenance as there was insufficient light to encourage the branches to regrow.

Ladies enjoying the shade of a tree arbour.

Tunnel Arbours /Pergolas

Tunnel Arbours were a common garden feature. The covered walkways allowed highborn ladies to take exercise without having to expose their skin to the elements and lose their highly prized, pale complexions. This was a status symbol, showing that they were ladies of leisure and did not have to work outside, becoming coloured by the sun and wind. Although it is possible that the ladies used chalk dust or creams as make-up for their faces, sheltering in an arbour would have been much safer than using the noxious substances which were the main ingredients of some of the cosmetics used to make the face appear white. Even Mary, a carpenter's wife, and the female saints are shown in paintings with white faces.

The construction of these arbours seems to develop from initially being bent poles bounded together to form a rounded tunnel, to sturdier structures made of worked wood. Unlike the popular modern living arbours, the withies shown in medieval

A lady walks in the cool shade of a tunnel arbour, enjoying the perfumed roses.

paintings do not appear to be of living wood. Later paintings of tunnel arbours show worked timbers, which would be stronger and longer lasting. The arbours are trained with roses or vines. As with the turf seats, the roses used are both red and white. The white roses, *Rosa* x *alba*, usually grow the tallest, compared to the smaller red roses, *Rosa gallica*. It is possible that the red roses could have been grafted onto the albas.

Flower Beds

The flower beds are most often shown as being raised and edged with wattle fencing, wooden planks or brick. The ninth century monk, Walafrid Strabo, meaning Walafrid the Squint-eyed, wrote a Latin poem, *Hortulus*, The Little Garden, where he described making his own raised beds, where he explained that he made raised beds so that the soil would not be washed away by the rain. He may have known from his reading that the Romans had made raised beds. There were other equally good reasons for doing this. Many castles and manors would have little soil within their walls. Archaeology has shown that the courtyard at the Prebendal Manor at Nassington had been covered with cobblestones by the reign of Richard II. This would reduce the amount of mud walked into the hall during the wet winter months. As there was now no soil within the

courtyard area, raised beds were a practical way of ensuring a suitable soil depth for the plants. Digging and weeding forks were not used during the medieval period; once the soil had been prepared it was best not to walk on it again. With raised beds you can work from the sides, which is shown in some manuscript pictures. The raised beds were square or rectangular and if the manuscript sources are reliable, the arrangement of the beds was made to suit the space available. The effect would be formal for most of the year, but the

Garden with flower beds, gravel paths and topiary. (Getty Image)

formality can be soon lost as the larger herbs grow through the season. Some authors describe the arrangement of the beds as like a chequer board, but there are paths between the beds.

There are no surviving instructions as to how the plants were to be arranged in the raised beds. The picture shows that the beds may not be uniform. There is a circular bed for the topiary with some of the square beds having small fences and others without. Some pictures suggest quite a lot of space between the individual plants, but whether there was a mixture of plants or each bed held several plants of the same type is not clear. Illustrations often show a lot of green over the surface of each bed. Was this meant to indicate the general foliage of plants, or grass with plants growing amongst it? Having experimented with both methods, I am inclined to think that it is the leaves of plants that is being shown. Growing flowering plants through the grass is not usually very successful and requires a lot of trimming to allow the plants to flourish and be clearly visible.

Paths

Paths within parks, orchards and vineyards were most likely to be of grass, but Lydgate's poem *The Churle and the Bird* says that the paths within the herbers were constructed using sand. This would be easy to keep smooth and level, and there would be no sharp stones to be felt through the thin-soled shoes of the period. Another advantage of sand is that it does not hold water and drains very quickly, so the visitors to the garden could have dry feet, as pictures do not show people in the garden wearing the typical clog-like pattens strapped to their shoes to keep their feet dry.

Pattens protected the soles of footwear. (Wiki commons)

Gloriettes and Summer Houses

Crescenzi said that your garden could have a gloriette that the lord and lady can retire to. It was a place where they could escape their duties and troubles and relax. If you were very wealthy, the gloriette would be built of stone. If you were not wealthy enough to afford a stone building, you may have a gloriette constructed using wood, but if you did not want to spend too much money, it could be made of wood and cloth, basically a tent.

You may also wish to plant a living building of trees. This was not a flimsy structure like the modern living willow structures that we are used to today. Crescenzi described the structure as having courtyards and having buttresses like a real building. This may not be just fancy. In the fifteenth century English poem, *Floure and Leafe*, the poet says that the garden is hedged with sycamore and eglantine and has a living roof so that it is a parlour of living plants, the walls being so thick, that you could walk around the outside all day without being able to tell whether or not anybody was inside.

A tent could provide a tranquil place of repose. (Wiki Commons)

Labyrinths and Mazes

A labyrinth has a continuous path that leads ultimately to the centre. There are no tricks or dead-end paths to confuse the person following the route. The path itself usually winds backwards and forwards so that an apparently small labyrinth can have a path that is several hundred metres long. Labyrinths are known to have existed for about 4,000 years. The early labyrinths have a cross shape within the layout that is near the entrance. Later Christian labyrinths have a cross form, that superimposes itself over the whole layout. During the medieval period, a labyrinth was more likely to be found on an open space such as a village green rather than in a garden, such as the one at Wing, Rutland, that is on the outskirts of the village.

A maze is intended to amaze and entertain you, or to make you walk, 'mazedly', so that you are not sure where you are going.

Mazes and labyrinths were certainly garden features during the Renaissance, as much for their formal layouts as their entertainment value. The late fifteenth century English poem, *The Assembly of Ladies*, tells of ladies entering a maze to pass the time, each having a different plan in mind as to how to reach the exit. Some were so 'mazed and confused' that they did not care which path they took. Others stood in the middle and looked around them for the best way. Some were so fed up, that they simply cheated and stepped over the rails, which suggests that there were no hedges to hide the view or to prevent a little dishonesty to find a way out again!

Labyrinth, Wing, Rutland.

Practical Garden Features

Kitchen Gardens

Manorial and monastic estates grew their own food in separate gardens from those for pleasure, but for most of the rural agricultural population and some of the inhabitants of towns, gardens would be mostly for producing food, with the decorative aspect being a secondary consideration.

At Nassington the main road through the village led to the gatehouse of the Prebendal Manor opposite the church, and there it originally stopped. On either

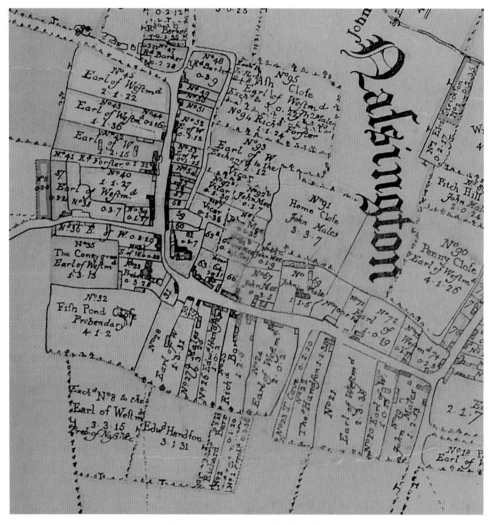

1778 Tithe Map showing the Prebendal Manor opposite the church and the garden plots along the road. Note Fishponds and Coneygarth for rabbits. (Northampton Records Office)

A GUIDE TO MEDIEVAL GARDENS

side of road were the villagers' houses; each house having a long, narrow plot of land behind it. The plots have survived to this day.

These gardens could be used for keeping pigs and growing the coleworts (the cabbage family), leeks, onions and garlic needed to flavour the pottage. The beans and peas would be grown in the fields in the three-field system. Peas and beans are both leguminous plants, having an additional advantage that not only do they provide food, but the roots of both plants have root nodules that fix nitrogen from the atmosphere in the soil. Nitrogen is the main nutrient that plants use to produce leaves and stems. There could be herbs flavouring, food, flax and maybe hemp, for the fibres in their stems, medicinal plants and possibly some dye plants. The beds could be set out in the back yard of the house, whether as raised beds or not. There could be

Medieval village gardens. (Wiki Commons)

fruit trees grown for fruit and shade, and maybe a turf seat to enjoy some relaxation from the daily toil. The Yeoman's Garden at the back of Bayleaf Farm at the Weald and Downland Museum, where although the house dates from the latter part of the medieval period, the garden has been planned to show a how a late medieval vegetable garden could have been set out. There are a series of rectangular beds that are used to grow examples of the food crops that were commonly used. It may often appear unruly to modern eyes, but many of the plants that a modern gardener may consider as weeds are edible or have some practical use. Fat Hen, *Chenopodium album*, is an annual plant that often gets into gardens with animal manure, has been used since very early times, and both the leaves and seeds are edible.

The beans, *Vicia faba*, are the plants that were used to breed from to produce our modern large seeded broad beans, but themselves would be more like the modern field beans grown as animal fodder. The seeds are much smaller but perfectly edible, even allowing for modern tastes. The Martock Bean originates from the village of Martock, Somerset and is said to have been rediscovered in the garden of the Bishop of Bath and Wells. It is thought to date from the twelfth century. Each plant can produce up to a hundred beans, making it very productive compared to other crops. Growing your own food may sound idyllic, but the reality of medieval life was the constant worry of whether your crops would grow. Even in a good year there were times between crops when food would not be plentiful, and you may have had to forage for wild plants. If your crops failed, you faced the prospect of starving. Whether it was a good year or not, ten per cent of your produce would be paid to the church as a tithe.

Dovecotes

In England a dovecote could only be built under licence from the king and was an extremely expensive building. The walls were about three feet thick to allow for the nesting holes. Dovecotes were usually able to hold some 500 pairs of birds. There are usually two chicks per clutch and depending on the weather, up to seven clutches per pair of doves in a year. This was factory farming medieval style. The surplus birds were sold in the local markets. Battle Abbey bought 794 pairs of doves in 1395–96 from the manor of Alciston for 44s 1d. The income for a dovecote, with 550 nesting holes, assuming you had seven clutches of eggs per year could be in the region of £15. The dung was used as a fertiliser and later the dung would be used to extract saltpetre, to be used for making gunpowder. Dove dung was also an ingredient for use in making some medicines. The birds would be eaten as squabs at around six weeks old, before they begin to fly and develop muscles. This makes them more tender to eat and saves a lot of firewood when it comes to cooking them. From practical experience, squabs cook in half the time it takes to cook an adult bird.

A GUIDE TO MEDIEVAL GARDENS

Dovecote, Prebendal Manor, Nassington.

Straw bee skeps.

Bees

Bees were kept for both honey and wax. The wax was added to oil to thicken ointments for medicinal use and for candles. Beeswax was expensive so only the church and the wealthy could afford to use beeswax for candles. Battle Abbey spent 16s for 22 lb of wax for candles and a suitable number of wicks. The honey was used as a sweetener, a medicinal ingredient and to make mead or metheglin, both being honey-based drinks.

The bees were kept in straw rope bound with split bramble stems. The hives, known as skeps, were usually destroyed in order to extract the honey, bees being easier to obtain in those days. There were many instructions on bee keeping that often drew on Roman techniques. With typical medieval misogyny, the queen bee was known as the king!

Vineyards

Vineyards were planted at many English estates and were part of the wider gardens. The monks of Bury St Edmunds were allowed to walk among the verdure of the vines after having been bled. It was considered that this would help calm them. Vines are mentioned in the bible on numerous occasions. Jesus told parables where he used the vineyard to illustrate his teachings. In one, Jesus refers to himself as the vine and he shows a certain amount of knowledge of tending vines when he talks of completely removing unfruitful branches and pruning the fruiting branches so that they will produce more fruit. The most potent symbolic feature of the grape was the red wine used during the mass that represented the very blood of Christ himself.

Vines were originally introduced into Britain by the Romans, and some vineyards seem to have remained in use once they left Britain because thirty-eight vineyards are mentioned in the Domesday survey.

Charlemagne asked that his vineyards should be cultivated correctly, and cuttings were to be sent to him for use elsewhere on his other estates. He also said that the wine presses should be properly maintained, and that nobody was allowed to use their feet to crush his grapes for making his wine. Later medieval paintings suggest that the idea did not catch on, because although wooden grape presses are shown, treading the grapes seems to have remained popular.

Rockingham Castle, Northamptonshire, had a vineyard from at least 1100, when Henry 1 spent 20s on it, and in 1130 he had more vines planted. During 1139/40, Stephen employed a vinedresser whose livery allowance was 30s with an extra 20s for him to buy whatever was necessary to maintain the vineyard. The vineyard was still there in 1440, because an inquisition valued it at 4s per annum.

A vineyard was planted at the Abbey of Ely by Abbot Brithnod in 1107, and William of Malmesbury rated the grapes grown at Ely Abbey as being only inferior to those being grown in Gloucestershire.

Vineyards were expensive to maintain. New poles that the vines were trained on would have to be cut to replace the rotten ones in the vineyard. The vines would be manured after the grapes had been harvested. Once the cold weather of winter had passed, the vines needed pruning before it became too warm or the vines would bleed, losing too much sap. The main stems had to be tied to supports, which involved the extra work of training and harvesting coppiced willow trees for withies or bark. As the grapes developed surplus leaves would be removed to allow the grapes to ripen, and once the grapes were ripe, it was time for the vendage, the harvesting of the grapes themselves. During 1313/1314, the man who looked after the vineyard that belonged to the castle of Higham Ferrers was paid 60s. The vineyard must have been productive because a 116 gallons of green must, probably the young wine produced from the vineyard grapes, were sold to the earl's household for 24s 10d. It was a profitable year as it only cost 4s 5d for the wages for thirty-eight men to harvest the grapes and to make the green must. As most of the European vineyards were in the once Roman empire the cultivation methods were probably similar and continued to be used. Cato and other Roman writers gave good descriptions on how to grow vines.

There were three main methods:

1. Training the vines into trees was a method used by the Romans and is shown in some medieval paintings, but was probably not common in Britain. The vine is naturally a climbing plant, so growing it into a tree is not as odd as may first be thought, but it does make harvesting the grapes difficult and I suspect that the yield and the quality was poorer than using the other methods. Ripening would also be more difficult in English vineyards.

2. Growing the vines as free-standing bushes is a method that is still commonly used in northern Spain. I tried this method of growing grapevines at the Prebendal Manor as part of an experiment to discover how many grapes the different methods of training the vines would produce, but the rabbits kept eating the new shoots, so I reverted to growing all of the vines using the pole system. Another drawback of growing vines as bushes is that although you have a small vine that is easy to prune, it does not allow for such full exposure of the grapes to the sun as when grown on poles and it also means a lot of bending down during the harvest.

3. Growing the vines on poles is the method most commonly shown in the medieval pictures. The poles were best made using the wood of alder trees as it is slow to

Vines grown as bushes in Northern Spain.

rot. The monks of Ely were proud of their vines. A monk wrote a poem describing Ely's vineyards, but he wrote that elm poles were used to support their vines. Both elm and alder woods are resistant to rotting.

'With joy the vine-branch bears its load: ripe grapes hang down;
Its leafage drapes the exultant ground, while up aloft,
The branches of an elm-tree elevate the vine.'

The trees that provided the wood for supports would be grown on your estate. Once established, the vines would be grown spiralled around the poles, which encourages lateral growths which can then be pruned to limit the number of leaves and bunches. Sometimes horizontal posts helped to provide more support and to encourage more bunches of grapes. Crescenzi wrote a whole chapter describing the cultivation of vines, the making of the wine and how to improve wine that has gone off. If the grapes did not ripen properly to make wine, the sour juice could be fermented to produce verjuice which was used for cookery.

Vines trained to poles.

Orchards

Orchards were an essential feature of early gardens, being of both a practical and a decorative use. They provide a mass of colour in the spring when little else would be in flower. The leaves provide shade from the heat of summer and later in the year there is the colour of the ripe fruit and the prospect of a good harvest.

Crab apples and pear trees can be found growing wild in Britain, but Crescenzi was aware that although wild fruit trees usually bear more fruits, they tend to be small and bitter, whilst cultivated fruit trees will bear fewer fruits but these are larger, better and more sweeter than those that the wild trees produce. The Romans brought the cultivated apple to England and introduced the idea of grafting trees and improving the taste and flavour of the fruits.

There were several sorts of apples available in medieval England, such as costard, blandarelle, permain and pippins. Coeur de Boeuf is a French variety of apple that is said to date from the thirteenth century and which is still available today.

Wardens were one of the commonest pears. They are quite hard and good for cooking. During the medieval period, water was not always reliably safe to drink, so people often drank some form of alcoholic beverage as a matter of course. Apples and pears were used primarily to produce cider and perry.

Coeur de Boeuf is said to be a medieval apple.

The St Gall plan suggests trees that you could grow in an orchard. The soft fruits that could be grown are, apples, pears, plums, figs, medlars, mulberry, service tree and quince, (*Cydonia oblonga*, not the Japanese quince, *Chaenomeles japonica*) .

Peach trees are also shown to be growing in the orchard. The peach trees were probably included by somebody who had seen them referred to in a copy of a Roman book. At that time, peaches could have only been grown with great difficulty in the northern regions of Europe, but we cannot be certain; somebody may have grown peaches in pots and protected them over the winter months. Nut trees were grown in the orchard cemetery: almonds, chestnuts,

Quince.

hazel and walnuts. Nuts provide a good source of protein that is easily stored, and oil can be extracted from the kernels. Laurel is also mentioned but as with other early gardening books, this means the bay tree, *Laurus nobilis*.

John Garlande, an Englishman living in Paris during the thirteenth century, listed the trees in his own orchard as: apples, cherries, pears, plums, quince, medlars, peaches, figs, chestnuts, almonds and filberts. There were also vines which he describes as being grown in ordered ranks and rows. John says that without these trees in his orchard, a rich man is reduced to beggary.

Crescenzi said that if you could not afford to have a pleasure park as a garden feature, then an orchard could be used in the same way. He gave details of how to measure the spacing between the trees in rows, and that walnut trees were not to be planted as they were considered to be unhealthy because of the noxious fumes that they supposedly gave off. He recommended cutting the grass in the orchard twice a year.

The orchard, as a substitute for a pleasure park, could be a haven to escape the cares of the world. The medieval English poem, *Pistil of Susan* tells us that:

'They play in the apple orchard
Whilst they might help Susan
To work away her woe.'

CHAPTER 6

Water in the Garden

Fountains

The Romans had developed elaborate water systems and fountains. In the city of Rome, wealthy citizens could pay to take water from that being brought into the city and utilise it to form pools, waterfalls and jets in their own gardens. Most of this technology was lost after the fall of the Roman Empire.

Medieval fountains are shown as being bowls or basins, as Albertus described them. Fountains were often similar in shape to the fonts that were to be found in churches. The water either bubbled up from the bowl or was taken to a height from where it was allowed to fall back into the bowl. Generally, jets of water spurting into the air would not return again until the renaissance. Some late medieval fountains are often shown as being tall and they could be very decorative, with fine moulding, similar in shape

Fountains add coolness and sound to a garden on a hot day at Tretower Court. (© Crown copyright (2020) Cadw)

to the surviving Eleanor Crosses. At the pilgrimage site of Holywell, in North Wales, you can still see a very fine medieval fountain. On the continent, medieval fountains can be seen at the Cluny museum in Paris and at some monasteries. Many are single pieces of stone with curved channels at the top for the overflowing water or lion-headed spouts to let the water flow into a pool below. At the Pope's Palace in Avignon, Pope Urban IV enclosed the orchard where he installed a large fountain of a Griffin. Pope Benedict XII had a large tank installed above the garden well, on the inner wall of the ramparts of the palace. The tank seems to have been filled by a water wheel that was constructed in 1334. It is thought that the tank was a reservoir for a fountain, which, to save water, would only be turned on when there were important visitors in the garden.

People are often shown bathing in fountains, singly or in groups. There seems to be no embarrassment even for the ladies who are surrounded by men.

The Manesse manuscript shows several garden scenes, including one of a man who is having an arm massaged as he is soaking in a medieval hot tub whilst being offered a goblet of wine and the ubiquitous rose chaplet.

One fountain that didn't exist, but we may wish that it did, is the fountain of Eternal Youth. You clamber into the fountain bent and elderly and emerge again fully restored to the prime of life!

Another small water feature was an enclosed spring. These are commonly shown, sometimes in open countryside, where they provided water for workers, wayfarers and animals. A spring or stream was enclosed with stone or even planks to contain the water. The Romances of the time frequently tell of spoons or beakers chained to the side

A man enjoys a hot soak in the garden. (By kind permission of Universitätsbibliothek Heidelberg)

of wells and fountains to make getting a drink easier, and such features are shown in the pictures too.

There are two wells similar to this design that may be possible medieval survivals, but if not, they are good representations of how such wells may have appeared.

One is Rosamunde's Bower, once known as Everswell, part of Woodstock Manor, Oxfordshire, a medieval hunting lodge that is now in the grounds of Blenheim Palace. The bower is named after Rosamunde Clifford, the mistress of Henry II. Henry is said to have kept his mistress safe within a labyrinthine bower to protect her from his understandably jealous wife, Eleanor. The story is that Eleanor spotted a loose thread that had caught on Henry's sleeve. She grabbed a bottle of poison and a dagger, followed the thread to Rosamunde and gave her the choice of how she would die. Rosamunde chose the poison and was buried at nearby Godstow Abbey. Aubrey sketched three successive enclosures of water within a walled garden. The story of poor Rosamunde must have had a Romantic appeal for the scholars at Winchester's Wykeham college as they had their own garden called *Rosemondesbour*, first mentioned in 1403. Unfortunately, sometime around 1740, Sarah Churchill ordered the final remains of Rosamunde's Bower to be removed, so there is only one to be seen today,

Rosamunde's Well, Blenheim.

St Winifride's Well, Woolston, Shropshire.

thanks to Capability Brown, who raised the level of the lake around Blenheim Place which submerged the site of the other two pools.

A similar feature can be seen at St Winifred's Well in Woolston, Shropshire. The well is said to have sprung from the resting place of the saint as her body was being carried to Shrewsbury Abbey. The spring rises from beneath the building and the water is reached by steps on the side. The building is dated to 1485 and was originally a chapel. It is now under the guardianship of the Landmark Trust and can be rented as a holiday home.

Wells

A well was essential for drinking water and the final siting of most properties would be reliant on a good supply of water for drinking, cooking, washing and industrial workshops. Springs are often referred to as wells or fountains, which can cause confusion over the exact meaning of what the writer intended. Wells to supply water for practical use were generally excavated down to the water table and lined to prevent the sides collapsing. To reach the water table, some wells were very deep; one well at Beeston Castle in Cheshire is 113 metres deep.

Decorative Well Head, Prebendal Manor.

A GUIDE TO MEDIEVAL GARDENS

Fishponds

Known as *stagnis* or *stanks*, ponds and pools were an essential feature for most manors and abbeys. They provided water for the breeding of fish and waterfowl. Ponds could supply drinking water for stock animals and allowed the growing of aquatic plants, such as watercress, mint and water lilies for culinary and medicinal uses, rushes for making rush lights and soft baskets or for strewing on clay and stone floors as insulation. Damp banks were ideal for growing willows to produce the long, thin, withies needed to make baskets and tie plants. But the most important use of a pond was for breeding fish. Medieval religious observance required fasting on all Fridays, most Wednesdays and Saturdays, all Holy Days and the day before them, the six weeks of Lent and the four weeks of Advent. This amounts to about half of the year being set aside for fasting when meat was not eaten, so fish became a major part of the Abbey's diet. Much of the fish for everyday consumption was salted or dried. It is now thought that the Abbey pools were used to breed the more prestigious fish such as bream, perch, pike, roach and tench, which were eaten on important feast days. Eels were commonly eaten, and many abbeys ran commercial fisheries from rivers running through their land. Water rights were important for food from fish and game birds, income and to power water mills.

Sometime after he had become the ruler of the Holy Roman Empire on Christmas day of the year ad 800, Charlemagne had a document drawn up, known as the *Capitulare de Villis*, which demonstrated the way that he wanted his estates in the Holy Roman Empire to be run. The *Capitulare* states that Charlemagne's stewards should maintain the fishponds on his estates where they had previously existed, to make them larger if practical, and where possible he wanted new fishponds to be made.

If not occurring naturally, ponds could be made by damming a river or stream. Another method was to dig a pit that would be lined or 'puddled' with clay to ensure that it retained the water. Fishponds may have been functional, but like orchards, they also had an aesthetic value, as they would in the later English landscape garden. Crescenzi suggested that your park could contain pools of water with fish as a pleasant attraction for visitors, but which could also be eaten. Pools and fish may also have held religious symbolism. The story of the loaves and the fishes, two of the essentials of a monk's diet, may have captured their imagination as Christ referred to himself as a 'fisher of men', and the first apostles were fishermen. Symbolism may have been the reason for having a piscina at Canterbury. The pool is very elaborate, having scalloped edges and what may be a decorative fountain in the centre. It seems to be fairly small too, so could never supply the necessary amount of fish required for food.

The Pope's Palace at Avignon has spectacular fourteenth century murals in the private study of Clement VI, which is usually known as the 'Chambre du Cerf', the Room of the Deer. The paintings completely cover the walls and depict rural scene of

Fishpond at Prebendal Manor.

hawking, hunting and fishing. One of the scenes shows a formal pool with many fish swimming within. Several men stand around the edge, fishing with nets and line. One of the fish is clearly shown as being a pike; the other fish would not survive for very long in that situation as the pike is a voracious predator.

In 1351 at Clare Castle, Suffolk, Lady Elizabeth de Burgh paid four pence to two little children to fish so she could watch them at play. Fishponds and moats would attract waterfowl which would provide food, entertainment from hunting them and would also be pleasant to look at and hear.

On many sites, there would be a series of ponds with the larger ponds, called the vivarium, used to breed the fish. Smaller ponds, referred to as a servatorium, were used for storing the fish shortly before they were to be used. To prevent stagnant water and keep the fish in a healthy condition, the water would need to flow, even if slowly,

Men fishing with a line and nets, Pope's Palace, Avignon. (Wiki Commons)

so the fishponds would need an inlet from a spring, river or stream. The medieval fishponds at the Prebendal Manor were fed and flowed back into the same brook, which eventually joined with the River Nene.

To produce fish long term the young fry would have to be protected in a separate pool so that the more mature fish could not eat them. The pike were kept away from the other fish for the same reason, in a pool known as the Jack Pond. In 1313/14 at Higham Ferrers in Northamptonshire, 6s 8d was paid for the wages of a fisherman whose job was to catch fish throughout the year to feed the pike. In the same period 59s 8d was paid for twenty-five pike and three score (sixty) tench to maintain the stock of the fishponds. It is likely that surplus fish were sold, but we cannot be certain.

Battle Abbey simply paid 2d to have their fishpond emptied so the fish could be collected before the arrival of the king, for whom they had to provide lodgings, along with his retinue.

Moats

The remains of medieval moats are dotted throughout Northern Europe.

Most were built between 1150 and 1325 for defence around castles or manor houses, the spoil from digging being used to help build defensive banks. Defensive moats were not always water-filled, but this did add an extra complication for an attacking force. Once cannons were in common use, castle walls could be pounded from a safe distance, so the moat would offer very little protection from attack. Moats are symbolic for the wealthy elite, implying the ability to pay for them and maybe a lineage going back to the Norman Conquest.

As well as for defence, a moat was a ready source of water. Drinking water would be supplied from wells, but moats could be used for bathing, washing clothes and for keeping fish. Moats would also encourage waterfowl, useful for food but also decorative. and perhaps it was not only at the Bishops Palace at Wells that swans were encouraged to ask for food by pulling a bell chain?

It is worth remembering that the castle's toilets would empty into the moat. Moats required a considerable expenditure to dig them, and this generally made them a high-status item. Recent research has led to the conclusion that the moats of later dates were also decorative, especially once the country had become more settled and less violent. Bodiam castle, Sussex, was built c. 1385 by Sir Edward Dalyngrigge using the profits of plunder from the wars in France. At first glance the castle seems to be everything a castle should be: there are stout walls and towers, a drawbridge, and with more defence from a vast system of moats and earthworks. But despite appearances, the castle, would be unable to defend itself for long if it had been besieged by a determined force armed with cannon. The castle was constructed with

The moat at Bodiam Castle was as much for show as defence.

large windows, which shows as much consideration for comfortable living as for defence, and the moats were built more for prestige than for protection. The large pond set below Framlingham castle in Suffolk is now recognised as being there for prestige and pleasure as much as for defence.

Moats were not only dug around buildings for defence and to display status; they could be used to prevent stock animals from straying or to protect gardens. Some orchards and pleasure parks were moated for privacy and to keep domestic animals in and wild ones out. Many moated compounds survive in Norfolk although their use is still uncertain. The surviving waterworks at castles such as Bodiam, Framlingham, Kenilworth and Leeds prove just how much money was being spent on landscaping the castle grounds and the amount of labour people were willing to expend on their creation.

CHAPTER 7

Parks and Pleasure Parks

Until fairly recently, medieval gardens were considered to be very small with turf seats, flowerbeds and arbours, and that because of the frequent outbreaks of violence, larger gardens would not be made until the more settled Tudor period. But recent research, including going back to original source material, has shown that this idea is inaccurate. The aristocracy had the resources, the finances and desire to make gardens on a large scale; this includes the pleasure park, which would not be as large as a hunting park, but would appear similar but treated much more as an extension of the pleasure garden.

The early deer parks were primarily a source of meat, yet they may have been used as park-like gardens. A twelfth century writer praised the woodland at Little Downham in the *Ely Lihellus*, where the delights of the park are rhapsodised:

> 'A green grove stands, well suitable for frequent hunts,
> Adorned with flowers and set about with banked-up turf,
> Enclosing in its ramparts every kind of beast.
> Here, while a sweet breeze wafts around, sings every bird:
> The chatting magpie, blackbirds, thrushes, turtle-dove
> And nightingales evoke harp-music as they sing,
> Competing with each other in loquacity.'

The enclosed woodland is suitable for hunting, but there are attractive plants and animals to admire and the song of birds to soothe the soul.

Chaucer and other poets use similar gardens as a setting for their writing, but the best description of them is by Crescenzi. For the wealthy and powerful he suggests the size of a park should be about twenty acres or more. Ideally the land would be flat and well-drained but with a flowing stream, and there should be no obstructions to allow plenty of fresh air to blow through. There should be a fine gloriette, a building constructed from stone or if that was too expensive, wood, where the king and queen or other lord or lady may retire to when they wish to escape from boredom and melancholy; it is a place to refresh their spirits.

The Little Park at Fotheringhay is to the south east of the castle and set back from the river Nene, just beyond an area of grassland shown as the 'laund' on a later map. It may have been created by the king during 1464, as he is recorded as having made a garden and a spinney to enclose the Little Park. It is one of the last places of high ground before the landscape falls and becomes the flat fenlands, so the views over the landscape would have been excellent. The Little Park covers twelve hectares, but besides the views it is ideally situated for the castle guards to maintain a discreet watch from the castle ramparts for maximum security. According to Crescenzi, a pleasure park should have a fishpond stocked with different types of fish for passers-by to admire. There should be friendly animals such as hares, rabbits, squirrels, deer and other herbivorous wild beasts. In

Part of the bank and ditch of Fotheringhay Little Park.

some of the trees close to the palace you could place cages of woven withies to hold pheasants, partridges, nightingales, blackbirds, linnets, goldfinches, canaries and other sorts of attractive birds that are good singers. Trees were to be planted to form ridings so that you could watch the animals crossing and grazing from the gloriette. This is a place to escape the worries of state and finance and to simply enjoy the natural world. Medieval paintings of Eden show the many different exotic animals that the wealthy of European countries wished to own, including lions and porcupines, although how well the more exotic animals would have survived is another matter. This is not just fanciful, wishful thinking. Charlemagne had wanted the stewards on his estates to keep swans, peacocks, pheasants, ducks, pigeons, partridges and turtle doves for ornament, although they were probably eaten as well. He was also the proud owner of an elephant, given to him by the fifth Abbasid Caliph of Persia, Harun al-Raschid, which amazingly survived for seven years.

Small pleasure park enclosed with hedges at the Prebendal Manor, Nassington.

A GUIDE TO MEDIEVAL GARDENS

The murals at Avignon show bird cages and in a painting of the Antwerp Guild of Archers a bird cage can be seen hanging in a tree. Peacocks are frequently shown in illuminations from the late fourteenth century onwards. Not only did they add an exotic decorative feature, but they also took pride of place at banquets. At this palace at Avignon, Pope Benedict 12th kept a lion that had been given to him by Robert of Anjou, King of Sicily, and Pope John 22nd kept exotic animals such as a lion and a camel, but also he had hardier beasts: a bear, boar, deer and wild cats. He was fond of peacocks and there were seventeen wandering the gardens, six of which were white. Elsewhere in France, John Garlande wrote that the king of France had a forest with apes, bears, lions, lynx, panthers, tigers, as well as the more common badgers, deer, foxes, otters, polecats, rabbits and squirrels. The chained monkey shown in the *Lady and Unicorn* tapestry would very likely have been found in some high-status gardens, as the monks at Battle Abbey paid 4d for a chain for their own pet monkey. In England, Henry I had a menagerie with exotic beasts at Woodstock. William of Malmesbury noted that the king was good at begging animals from foreign kings, so that he was able to acquire camels, lions, leopards and lynxes, and William of Montpellier gave him a porcupine. Henry would have also had other friendly animals in the form of rabbits. Rabbits were possibly introduced by the Romans, but if so, were later re-introduced by the Normans. The rabbits were carefully managed in a conygree to provide meat and fur and did not escape from the parks to become wild in the countryside until the late fifteenth or early sixteenth centuries. A conygree has survived in a field not far from the church at Fotheringhay. It is a long mound with a moat around the outside. The moat was probably filled with water as a deterrent, with the hope that the rabbits would not escape.

Medieval rabbit warren, Fotheringhay.

Hunting Parks

During the medieval period there were two landscapes. The one tended by man, where there were fields of tended crops, coppiced woods and parks for deer and other animals. The implication of which is man governing nature, not nurturing it in its true state; this land is safe and controlled. Things were more insecure beyond the cultivated land, where you would find its antithesis, the Wild Wood. The deserted and uncultivated wilderness was a landscape of mystery and magic, where strange mythical beasts and spirits roamed. It was the place where a questing knight would go in search of adventure. More prosaically, it was the haunt of outlaws and others who wished to escape the over-bearing feudal system where they were held in bondage, mortally by the lords and spiritually by the church.

Hollywood films may give the impression that hunting ranged across country with lords galloping on their horses, huntsmen blowing on horns and the baying of hounds, but most hunting took place in parks. The parks were practical, but they were a designed landscape that would be attractive too. Parks were a statement of wealth and power. Theoretically you paid the crown for a licence to 'empark', to enclose the land. You then had to possess spare land needed to make your park, although the land chosen for parks was usually the least productive because you did not want to waste good farmland. The park would need enclosing with banks around the outside which could be surmounted with fencing pales or hedges.

The best plant to provide a fast-growing and impenetrable hedge still is hawthorn, *Crataegus mongyna*. It can be allowed to grow for a few years and then laid to make

Deer park, pale fencing of split chestnut wood at Charlecote Park.

it impossible for larger animals to pass through it. Another method was to grow it for two years and then cut it back to just above the ground, creating dense growth from ground level. The maintenance required to keep the boundaries secure was quite high. Traces of the double banks and ditches of the Great Park can still be seen on the outskirts of Fotheringhay village.

New locks for the gates into the park were another regular expense. The park is not just woodland; scrub was needed for small game animals and birds to hide, and open grass areas, known as 'launds', were essential for grazing animals. A forest or chase were much the same as a park, but they were not enclosed. Having enclosed your park, you then had to buy the deer from the king because in England the deer were all owned by the king, who would give or sell deer to his lords to stock their parks for hunting. If you had served the king well, he may have donated some deer to you. Deer leaps that allowed wild deer into your park from the wild, but prevented their escape, were illegal unless granted by the king. It was not only the aristocratic lords who owned parks, and many of the abbeys, such as Peterborough, made deer parks as a status symbol and to entertain their secular guests. Although hunting deer was tightly controlled, the local residents usually had right of access to the parks for grazing and wood. Deer were sometimes granted as a favour; the prebendary at Nassington was allowed one buck and a doe a year from Fotheringhay Great Park.

Parks were designed to visually impress people besides being practical. In the story of *Gawain and the Green Knight*, the castle of Sir Bertilak was set in a meadow, surrounded by a moat, with the park all around. The park was enclosed by a spiked pale fence with closely spaced spikes to stop people entering. Gawain thought that the fence must be two miles long. The maintenance of the hedges and fences was expensive. At Higham Ferrers, the man who repaired the park hedges was paid 5s for a year to make sure they remained impenetrable. The cost of materials was extra!

Besides their use for hunting, parks and woodland were maintained to produce timber for many different uses. The peasant's home was generally built with wooden frames, infilled with wattle that would be covered with daub. The roof of a low status building was mostly thatch, but higher status building could be roofed using shingles made of split wood, which then had to be smoothed and which made them more expensive. Wood was needed in large amounts for the fires at the manor for cooking and heat. The thicker wood was cut to make logs, the branches were tied in bundles as faggots to heat the ovens and smaller twigs were used as kindling.

The church did not take kindly to people who took timber from its woods. In 1318, Worcester cathedral decreed that several men who had taken wood illegally be stripped to their shirts and made to walk barefoot in a procession before High Mass, each carrying a candle of one pound in weight, which they were to offer at the altar. If any of them were priests, they would not have to strip or walk in bare feet.

Coppiced hazel provided wood for fencing, hedge-laying and thatching.

A GUIDE TO MEDIEVAL GARDENS

Wood was used to make spoons, bowls, drinking vessels, barrels, furniture, musical instruments, pattens to be worn on the feet, handles for tools, ploughs, fencing, poles for the vines and other plant supports, baskets, wind and water mills, ships, bows, arrows, shields, weapon handles and animal accoutrements. Acorns and beech mast and the thinner branches were used for animal feed. Elm, which resists rotting, was used for water pipes and vine supports.

Coppiced poles had many uses. Coppicing is where trees are cut to ground level, producing many new stems, which can then be harvested every four to seven years or so, depending on the species. Newly coppiced trees needed protection from deer and other grazing animals that will eat the tender new growth, so brush wood was used to make dead-hedges to keep them out. Another advantage of coppicing is that the trees can live much longer than a tree left to grow naturally. Pollarding is the coppicing of trees at above head-level, so that the new shoots are protected from grazing animals. Within the coppice, oak trees could be planted, spaced out to allow them to grow with straight trunks. These standard oaks were left to grow into mature trees and were prized for building materials such as roof beams and the central pole of windmills. Oak will also stand coppicing and pollarding.

Ash burns well, fresh or dried. It is too flexible to be useful as a building material and it is often attacked by beetle. The flexibility made ash very useful as the shaft or handles for hand tools and weapons. Ash was used to make the frames and shafts of carts. For domestic use, ash was good for making cups, bowls and plates as it doesn't taint the contents. Ash provided archers with the best arrow wood, but it only makes a second-rate bow.

Beech was used for fuel, cups, bowls and chairs. During the autumn, pigs could be taken into the woods to fatten them on beech mast before being slaughtered for the winter. Hazel does not break when twisted, making it ideal for wattle fencing and hurdles. Roof thatchers use hazel to make the twisted U-shaped spars that fix the horizontal hazel rods that hold the thatch in place on the roof. Hazel was also split and used to bind the spars to hold wooden vessels such as small barrels, tankards and buckets together as it was effective and cheaper than metal bands. Coppiced wood was used to make charcoal, whilst the brushwood was bundled into faggots. Hazel also provided nuts, if the squirrels didn't get them first. Hornbeam was pollarded for fuel, especially around the London area. Birch was coppiced for fuel, but the smaller branches weren't wasted as they were ideal for making besom brooms. Alder is another light wood which was grown to make vine supports and other posts. Alder wood resists water, so the poles would have a long useful life. During the reign of Henry VIII, the arrow makers were given preferential treatment in the use of ash. This upset the makers of pattens, wooden footwear similar to clogs, who were now banned from using ash and forced to use alder instead; alder only being a second-rate arrow wood.

CHAPTER 8

The Plants of the Medieval Garden

Flowers were much-loved during medieval times. They glow in stained glass windows, proclaimed family and hereditary lines in heraldic achievements, they were embroidered onto clothing, embossed into leather, cast as expensive gold and silver vessels, painted onto manuscripts and walls and carved in stone and wood. They were a part of everyday life.

Plants are the finery of a garden and the manner in which they are planted and maintained affects the overall appearance and atmosphere of a garden. It is through the changes in the plants that we readily observe the changing seasons. Most of the plants grown in the medieval garden are what we often now refer to as herbs, but in the past, herb was the word to describe a plant, not one that was essentially useful. Knowing which plants were grown in Britain during the medieval period is not always easy; for although we have a few lists of the plants that were known at the time, it is still difficult to decide

Lady surrounded by flowers. (Ripple church)

which plants were being grown. Herbals, which describe plants that were used in medicine, are not an indicator of what was actually being grown in Britain. Most herbals were copies of classical texts with many of the plants originating in the Mediterranean region and beyond, and many of the plants would not have survived easily in Britain. Many plants for food, medicine and practical use had been imported into Britain since at least the Roman period. They were necessarily grown here. Another problem is that although the herbals provide plant names, these are not always useful as a guide to finding the correct modern botanical name. Even into the Tudor period and often beyond, the common plant names tend to confuse the modern historian, who is rarely a botanist. For example, iris were often referred to as lilies. The earlier illustrations were not always very accurate either and the descriptions of the plants could be equally confusing for somebody who did not personally know the plant being described. For example, the *Agnus Castus* herbal gives a good description of the Affodilla:

'Affadilla is an herb that people call bell bloom. It is like leek and it has a yellow flower. It has a round seed head that has seed like onion seed.'

Many people may think of a daffodil, but from the description alone, the author may have been referring to the yellow asphodel; the description applying equally well to both plants.

The earliest list of plants from England is known as *Aelfric's List*, a Latin and Early English grammatical exercise in vocabulary. On one side of the page there is a list of plants written in Latin, and on the other, the Saxon translation. Whether these plants were grown in England we cannot be sure. We do not even know if the scribe had ever seen the plants. The document is an educational tool, not a horticultural treatise.

Another early plant list is found in Charlemagne's *Capitulare de Villis*, being a list of plants and trees which he wants to be grown on his estates. Most of the plants are edible but it includes those of medicinal use and for textile production. Yet it is only a list and no information is given as to how the plants are to be grown or for their uses.

In his poem, *Hortulus*, c.842, Walafrid Strabo talks of the joy that comes from tending a garden, and unlike the classical authors, Walafrid was speaking from practical experience. The pleasant garden by his door had once been a wasteland with puddles and overgrown. He tells us of the work needed to prepare his soil and then goes on to describe how to grow twenty-five plants and gives their uses. Sadly, Walafrid did not die a peaceful death in his garden; he drowned attempting to cross the River Loire in 849. The *Capitulare* and Strabo both include iris, lilies, and roses, leading some writers to suggest that the plants were grown mainly for their beauty, but all three of them could be grown for entirely practical uses.

The rose petals were used to produce rose oil and rose water. The dried and powdered rhizomes of *Iris florentina* were known as Orris powder, and lily bulbs could be eaten as a vegetable or used to make a cough medicine.

The Orris Iris, Iris florentina, was grown for its rhizomes and flowers.

The German, Abbess Hildegard von Bingen, 1098–1179, is more well-known today for the music that she wrote for her nuns, but she also wrote a book about medicine that includes ingredients from metals, minerals, animals, birds and fish as well as plants for her remedies. She appears to be writing from practical experience as well as the classical authors. Many of the plants could have been grown wild locally, others could be grown in gardens, whilst other exotic plants would have been bought. The book includes food plants and medicinal ones, although all plants have medicinal uses.

There were people writing about the plants being grown in some English gardens. Alexander Neckam was Abbot of Cirencester in 1213. Chapter 166 of his book, *De Naturis Rerum*, written in prose, describes trees, herbs and flowers grown in gardens. *Laudibus Divinae Sapientae* is a poem, of which part seven is about plants and part eight is about crops and trees. In all about 140 species are listed. Both books were popular throughout the medieval period. Bartholomew de Glanville, 1200–1260, wrote a book on gardening based on Pliny's writings that included his own observations. Henry the Poet, c.1235–1313, describes a square garden, set out as if it were within a cloister. He lists nearly 100 plants that he is growing, with about twenty-five on each of the sides.

A recreation of Henry the Poet's garden at the Prebendal Manor, Nassington.

His list includes some plants that modern readers may wish to leave growing in the wild, such as nettles and bindweed. Henry Daniel was a Dominican friar who was living in England c.1375. He wrote *Aaron Danielis*, which consists of two parts: *De re Herbaria* and *De Arboribus*. Henry refers to a garden which he once had at Stepney, London, where he grew 252 different sorts of plants.

John Gardener wrote a poem, now known as *The Feate of Gardenynge*. The surviving manuscript dates to about 1440 but may have been written earlier. The poem is a calendar of tasks to be carried out in the garden and mentions about 100 herbs and vegetables. The plants that he suggests growing tend to be more practical rather than decorative. It is thought that John was possibly a master gardener at the royal palace of Westminster or at Windsor Castle. It has been said that the poem is a great insight into medieval horticultural methods, but although it describes grafting, successional sowing, and how to take vine cuttings, there is little else about gardening methods. He does provide the first mention in England of planting saffron. What we can be certain of is that the information given is sound, practical advice that will produce good results if followed. With these lists we have a good idea of what was or could have been growing at the time. There are about 250 different plants mentioned, although many common wildflowers are not included, so there may have been more choice than is actually recorded.

Some plants are reputed to have been introduced into England during the medieval period. The Findern Lily, *Narcissus poeticus*, is said to have been taken to the village of Findern, in Derbyshire, by Geoffrey de Fynderne when he returned from fighting in the crusades.

Eleanor of Castile is thought to have brought hollyhocks to England, along with some Spanish gardeners to tend her plants and gardens. Archbishop Thomas Becket is often alleged to have brought a fig tree with him from Rome to England, which was planted in the garden of his palace at Tarring, Sussex. St Richard of Chichester is also cited as introducing the figs.

Wallflowers may have come over with Norman building stone. The Saxons tended to build in wood, but after the conquest, the Normans replaced many Saxon buildings with stone ones. It was easier to transport stone by water, rather than overland using carts, so they imported stone by sea from places such as Caen. Wallflower seeds came over with the stone; wallflowers can still be seen growing on the walls of Newark Castle and at numerous abbeys ruins. These wallflowers are smaller and not so heavily scented as the Siberian hybrids that we grow in our gardens today. Meanings and symbolism can change over time; today, to be a wallflower is to be too shy to dance and to sit out the fun. In medieval times it represented faith in adversity and undying love.

Narcissus poeticus, the Findern Lily.

A saffron flower showing the precious stamens.

The spice saffron is the dried threads of the stigmas of *Crocus sativa*, a plant that may have originated in Iran, Greece or Mesopotamia. Saffron is still very expensive because there are only three stigmas on each flower, and they have to be carefully removed by hand. Saffron was a major source of income for the Arabs, who knew it as *za'faran*, meaning yellow, the dye being used for cloth and manuscript paints. Besides its use as a food flavouring and colourant, it was used medicinally. Saffron was a plant that the Arabs wished to keep to themselves because of its value; for example, in 1275 the cellarer of Battle Abbey bought one ounce of saffron for 9s 8d. But the price varied considerably during the medieval period, as in 1278/78 Brother Nicholas was able to buy 3 lb of saffron for 18s; by 1320/21 the price had fallen and Brother John was now able to buy 2 lb for only 7s, but Brother Robert Bregg in 1371–72 found that prices had soared again as he had to pay 61s for only 3 lb of saffron! It is often said that saffron had been brought to England by a pilgrim to the Holy Land, who smuggled it out of the country by hiding a single corn in his staff, but this is mostly likely just a romantic story.

The *Romance of the Rose* suggests that foreign plants were being imported into Europe to improve the gardens and as a display of wealth:

'Every tree, from out the land of Saracens
He brought, for well he knows the art
To make his garden a delight.'

This may have been the case of the poet exaggerating, but we cannot be certain because there is an unusual example of 1297, when a document, the *Compotus of Kettering*, records that olive trees were bought for planting at a cost of 4d. The number of trees is not given, but this must be one of the earliest records of olive trees being grown in England.

Vegetables and Herbs

Both religious and secular estates also needed utility gardens to produce food and flavourings, medicines, textiles and dyes. There would have to be areas for the growing of vegetables and herbs. Vegetables were not just food but were used as medicines to help keep your humours in balance. Cold foods such as lettuce would be used to reduce the heat of hot humours.

Although it used to be said that the upper classes of medieval period did not eat vegetables the surviving recipe books would suggest otherwise. There are many

Medieval vegetable garden.

accounts for the buying of seeds to grow vegetables too. John Gardener says that you should plant 'wyrtys', the medieval name for cabbages, for both master and knave, clear evidence that the upper classes were eating their greens.

The cabbage family was part of the staple diet, but it is difficult to know for certain what was available. Cabbage was probably introduced by the Romans and can be found growing wild on the south coast and other places. Wild cabbage is more like kale than the headed cabbages that we are used to today. There may have been other forms of cabbage because red and white cabbages are both included in William Caxton's book, *Dialogues*. This was a French and English phrase book and vocabulary. The *Ménagier* talks of five types of cabbage. Headed Roman cabbages were harvested in the autumn to eat over winter. The stems were then pulled up and replanted elsewhere and allowed to grow small heads, which he called sprouts. There were Easter cabbages for eating in the spring. Winter leaves were best eaten after a frost, but all cabbages were to be cooked for a long time over a strong fire.

In Langland's book *Piers the Ploughman*, we learn about the food that the peasants were eating. There were plenty of cabbages, shallots, onions, green leeks, parsley, beans and peas which were eaten as pease pudding. Peas and beans were dried for winter use rather than being eaten fresh. They are a good source of protein, that once dried, can be easily stored over winter. They may get nibbled by pests, but that would not be a major problem.

Peas and beans were often added to grains to make bread if the crops were not good or you were short of money. The lower classes ate pottage as one of their main meals of the day, as they would for centuries to come. This is a thick soup with seasonal vegetables and herbs with whatever else you could add.

The onion family was one of the major flavourings for food. Both red and white bulb onions are mentioned in documents. Onions and shallots were one of the main ingredients of pottage. Garlic is strongly flavoured, a good antiseptic and was thought to be good for curing just about

Wortys and leeks.

A GUIDE TO MEDIEVAL GARDENS

everything. Chives are useful as a milder flavouring. Welsh onions or scallions, used the same way as chives, provide leaves all year, but especially over the winter months.

Leeks are easy to grow and with care you can have leeks nearly all year. Most were sown broadcast, simply scattered across the soil and known as green leeks. Others were sown in trenches, much as we would today. These were known as white leeks and were more expensive and probably a higher status food as they require more space and effort to grow them well. As with many of the leafy vegetables it was grown as a 'cut-and-come-again' plant. You remove the leaves as you need

Beans were a good source of protein.

them, rather than cutting off the whole plant. This saves the effort of the constant re-sowing for new plants and the extra labour of watering young plants. Beets, spinach, wild celery grown for its leaves, not stems, Good King Henry, *Chenopodium bonus-henricus*, and the native wild plant, salad burnet, *Sanguisorba minor*, were all grown as leaf vegetables. Lettuce is a native plant of Britain, but the wild lettuce is very bitter to taste and was used as a sedative. Pictures of the time show a cos-type lettuce for food, which had probably been bred by the Romans. Parsnips and radish were the main root plants, but the short, thin roots of skirrets (*Sium sisarum*) had been eaten by the Romans. The Emperor Tiberius loved them, and they are mentioned in some medieval plant lists. Carrots were possibly introduced as a result of the crusades; our native white rooted carrot rarely produces a very large root, but it was possibly eaten during the many hungry periods.

Carrots could be stored in barrels or boxes of sand kept in a dry, cool cellar or barn. The colour of earlier carrots could vary considerably, being white, yellow, orange, red or purple.

These colours are now readily available again in most supermarkets. Orange carrots are said to have been made popular by the Dutch to show loyalty to William of Orange, but they are also the favoured colour for manufacturers of canned and bottled carrots because they keep their colour better than others when processed.

Many of our common weeds could be collected from the wild for food rather than grown in the garden. It is hard to know which so-called weeds may have been grown,

Carrots came in more colours than just orange.

especially when John Gardener says that he is intentionally growing groundsel, *Senecio vulgaris*, and Herb Robert, *Geranium robertianum*, which was named after the founder of the Cistercians and was one of the many plants that it was believed would cure the plague.

Plants provided dyes for cloth and some of the colours for paints. Rose Madder, *Rubia tinctorium*, is related to goose grass and gives a red dye from its roots, which need to be at least three years old before harvesting. The best madder was said to come from the cliffs near Athens. Weld, *Reseda luteola*, is a tall annual plant whose leaves can give yellow or green.

Dyer's Greenweed, *Genista tinctoria*, is a broom-like shrub that gives a yellow dye from its branches and leaves. Woad, *Isatis tinctoria*, was made famous by Julius Caesar's remark about the ancient British using it to paint themselves blue. It has been found by archaeologists at King's Lynn and York. The process to extract the blue dye from the leaves involved fermented human urine and caused the dyers to smell and have blue hands, so the dye families had to inter-marry as nobody else would have them. Onions skins would have been in plentiful supply and are easily dried and stored. You can use them to produce a range of colours from yellow through orange to a rich brown. All the colours can be adjusted by over-dying and using different mordants that are added to fix the colours in the cloth. The material from which the dye-pot was made will affect the final colour; an iron dye-pot will produce a much darker colour than an earthenware one.

A GUIDE TO MEDIEVAL GARDENS

Plants were grown to produce textiles. The annual flax with blue flowers, *Linum usitatissimum*, was mostly grown to make linen thread and cloth. The seeds produce linseed oil. Linen cloth is much easier to clean than woollen cloth, so was useful for making shirts and undergarments worn next to the skin. Hemp, *Cannabis sativa*, was grown for its fibres and is recorded in several plant lists and financial accounts. The fibres may have been used to produce sewing threads rather than clothing and to make nets for hunting birds and game.

The fibrous stems of stinging nettles could be used in a similar way.

Fuller's Teasel, *Dipsacus fullonorum*, was grown for its hard, spiky heads which were used to brush on woollen cloth to raise the knap. The heads are

Dye plants are often decorative as well as useful.

much stiffer than the teasel that is usually found growing wild.

The roots of soapwort, *Saponaria officinalis*, produce a soft colourless soap that was used for washing clothing. The plant is very vigorous and spreads rapidly, so it is easy to grow enough for use and still have roots left over to grow more plants.

Several plants were used to flavour drinks. Mugwort, ground ivy and alecost were used to flavour ales before the introduction of hops.

The medicinal use of plants was recorded in the herbals or passed on verbally. Many of the medicinal plants had other uses too. Caper spurge, *Euphorbia lathyrism*, is a violent purge, used to help balance the humours of the human body, which would help to keep a person healthy. Pertelote, the hen in Chaucer's *Nun's Priest Tale* uses the plant to help cure the bad dreams that her husband, the cockerel Chanticleer, is suffering from.

The floors of houses were often strewn with rushes for insulation, which could encourage bugs and bad smells. Plants such as tansy, rue, fleabane and wormwood could be added to deter pests from the floor covering, but also to remove worms from your innards. One story tells how the shepherds who went to Christ's crib added thyme and pennyroyal to the straw to scent Christ's stable and keep the bugs under control.

Some plants have less obvious uses. Bracket fungus was imported by ship into London from Germany during the fifteenth century by the trading organisation, the Hanseatic League, as tinder to light fires.

Hemp was grown to produce fibres.

Symbolism and Plants

Flowers were a popular subject in medieval art, painted in manuscripts, stained glass windows, walls and panels in buildings and as part of the heraldic achievements of the elite. Plants were sewn to decorate clothing, woven into tapestries and carved in stone over doors and ceilings in wood for roof bosses, misericords and bench ends.

Flower motifs were used to decorate homes.

A GUIDE TO MEDIEVAL GARDENS

Roses

Initially the church did not look on roses favourably as they were associated with the goddesses of carnal love, Aphrodite and Venus, and the excesses of the Roman Empire, but you cannot stop people loving roses, so they soon acquired Christian symbolism. One medieval myth told how roses originally had white flowers until the crucifixion. In this story the crown of thorns was made of a flowering rose briar. Christ's blood stained the flowers red, so that the red rose became symbolic of Christ and the blood of the martyrs. The white rose represented Mary and purity. The red rose bud came to represent Christ, and later, the beloved in secular Romantic writings.

The Annunciation scene in the Ramsey Psalter, now held in the Morgan library, shows the archangel Gabriel approaching Mary to tell her that she will give birth to Christ. Instead of the usual Madonna Lily, the artist shows a pot of red roses, hinting at Christ's death as a martyr.

The red rose was *Rosa gallica var. officinalis*, the Apothecary's Rose. It was said to have been taken to France by Thibaut IV in 1240 when he returned from the crusades. It was grown at Provins, near Paris. The petals keep their scent when dried, making them useful for pot pourri. They were also distilled to produce rose oil and rose water for medicines, food flavourings and cosmetics.

Rosa gallica var. officinalis, the medieval red rose, was beautiful but had many practical uses.

The multi-coloured Rosa Mundi.

The rose can often produce a sport, a shoot, that produces a red flower with white streaks, the rose known as *Rosa Mundi*. This is often grown in recreated medieval gardens, but it is neither mentioned in documents nor shown in paintings until much later, far too late for it to have been realistically named after the Fair Rosamunde, Rosamunde Clifford the mistress of Henry II. Graham Thomas proposed the idea that a crusader knight found the rose in Syria and gave it to Rosamunde, but it seems unlikely.

People have always wanted to have flowers when they are not naturally in season. In earlier times this would be a way to show off your wealth and status. The Romans imported out of season roses from Egypt at great cost, but if you wanted to have roses in winter during the fourteenth century, the *Ménagier* had a method. During the summer you should pick rose buds with long stems and put them in a small wooden barrel. The barrel should then be sealed and bound so that it is completely watertight. Then tie a large and heavy stone to each end of the barrel and lay the barrel in a running stream until you want the rose. An English manuscript suggests that you can encourage early flowering of roses by planting them close together and carefully moistening the stems with hot water.

There are several roses native to Britain. The most common is the Dog Rose, *Rosa canina*. The Hildesheim Rose in Germany was said to have been planted when the

Eglantine Rose.

Hildesheim cathedral was first built, c. 815. The rose, which is a Dog Rose, survived bombing and fire during the Second World War and now attracts many visitors who want to see what is alleged to be the oldest cultivated rose bush in Europe.

Eglantine, *Rosa eglanteria*, is mentioned in several texts. The flowers are not scented but the leaves are, giving off a scent similar to that of green apples if the leaves are crushed slightly or as the dew dries in the morning.

The Burnet Rose, *Rosa pimpinellifolia*, is a self-suckering plant with petals that mostly range from white, to cream and to pale yellow. The scent has a hint of lemon. It grows at the Abbey ruins at Dunwich, Suffolk and is said to have survived since the medieval period. Because it uses suckers to produce new shoots and is not a grafted plant it is quite possible that this is so, especially as the rose likes coastal regions.

There were many flowers dedicated to Mary, not only white ones, but those that were especially attractive or had a pleasant scent. Many of the flowers are shown with Mary in her *Hortus Conclusus*. Violets were for purity and modesty but could be used medicinally. Marigolds were known as Mary's Golds, and could be used medicinally or as the common name, Pot Marigolds, suggests, go into the cooking pot, although the flavour is rather strong for modern tastes. The petals could be rolled and dried as an adulterant of saffron, which is a dodge that is still used today.

Burnet Rose.

The white marks of the thistle Silybum marianum are symbolic of the milk of the Virgin Mary.

Mary's Thistle or Holy Thistle, *Silybum marianum*, has white markings on the leaves that are to remind you of the milk of Mary, but it has medicinal uses and can still be bought at chemists today.

Clematis is a vigorous climber that could easily be trained over arbours and was known as Our Ladies Bower. Sweet woodruff became Our Lady's Lace but had a practical use as a strewing herb, because the dried leaves have the scent of new-mown hay. Foxgloves were Our Lady's Gloves, and harebells became Our Lady's Thimbles.

Not all the flowers were associated with Mary. Cowslips were called St Peter's keys. A myth tells how St Peter became so annoyed by people trying to enter heaven by the back gate that he accidentally dropped the keys, which fell into a cloister garth where they grew as cowslips.

Plants and Flowers; Rents and Rewards

The bible mentions herbs as payment for tithes when Jesus argues with the Pharisees, noting that they pay their tithes of cumin, dill, mint and rue. This may have been the inspiration for similar payments during the medieval period when plants were used as payment or part-payment for tithes and rents of land or property. This seems to have been a fairly common practice, although mostly in the form of cumin, peppercorns and roses.

Pepper was an expensive spice and is often mentioned in contracts to rent property, hence our term, peppercorn rent. This would have been a rent of considerable value, not the token gesture that a peppercorn rent, where we tend to think of a single peppercorn, would suggest today.

Joan Patrick of Nassington, Northamptonshire, was owed rent of two pairs of gloves, a pound of cumin and three roses for the village of Carlton, near Rockingham.

At the Prebendal Manor, Nassington, Northamptonshire, a document dated 20 March in the 29th year (1450) of the reign of Henry VI, records rent paid for a vineyard:

'...and half a pound of pepper rent from the prebendary of the prebend of Nassington for a garden called the vineyard.'

Another unpaid pepper rent was also due at Nassington on the same day:

'And also for a half pound of pepper rent from John Sayten' p.a. not received as he settled on the hearing day, the above account for his fee.'

The Gold Rose at the Cluny Museum. (Wiki Commons)

One of the most extravagant rose gifts was the golden rose that the Pope would give on the fourth Sunday of Lent, also known as Rose Sunday, to a king, prince or princess to whom he wished to show particular favour for services rendered.

The Cluny Museum in Paris has the oldest surviving golden rose, which was given to the Count of Neuchâtel by Pope John XXII in 1330. The rose has gold petals, stems and leaves. One flower has a sapphire in the centre, the other flowers may have originally, but not now. Henry VIII was the last English monarch to receive a golden rose from the Pope.

Surprisingly, a rose rent is still being paid to Sir William Clopton of Toppesfield Manor, Hadleigh, Suffolk. Clopton granted a Market House and the land to build the Guildhall with all the market rights to the town of Hadleigh, Suffolk, in 1438. The rent was originally one mark a year, but this was later altered to one red rose, the most likely rose being *Rosa gallica 'Officinalis'*. The rent eventually became forgotten until 1984, when Gene Clopton noticed that the rent had not been paid to his family for many years, asked for settlement. The rent is now paid by the Mayor of Hadleigh every year by placing a red rose on the tomb of Sir William at the church of the Holy Trinity at Long Melford. The last time I was there, the rose was an artificial one, but it is good to see that an effort has been made.

Sir William Clopton with his rose rent, Long Melford.

CHAPTER 9

The Medieval Gardener

Early in the medieval period the gardener was most probably a labourer tied to a manor, carrying out gardening and agricultural work. His hours would have varied considerably according to the season. Walter of Henley, who wrote a treatise on looking after your land, estimated that you should allow eight weeks for Holy Days and other hindrances when planning the work on your estate.

On many estates the women and children certainly carried out much of the weeding and simple tasks such as planting and weeding leeks as their pay was usually half of that paid to a man. This was still common practice in the eighteenth century, as the accounts for Apethorpe Manor, Northamptonshire, record that four women were regularly employed to do the weeding in the gardens.

Royal and monastic gardeners are recorded as earning more than the general labourers, so it is likely that they were supervising the manual labourers who were actually carrying out the practical gardening tasks.

We do not know the training given to medieval gardeners, but an early form of The Worshipful Company of Gardeners is a modern survival of the guilds that could be found in each town or city; the current guild dates from the late nineteenth century. The Worshipful Company of Gardeners is first recorded in August 1345 in the archives of the Corporation of London, when a fellowship of gardeners made a petition to the Lord Mayor to allow them to return to a market site next to the old St Paul's cathedral; they had been forced off the site because of the noise they created which had disrupted the lives and services of the monks in St Austin. The gardeners failed in their petition, but they were instead granted the use of two other sites at Bayard Castle and Cheapside. The gardeners were those employed by the 'Earls, Barons and Bishops and the Citizens of the City of London' and were organised enough to put forward their demands and get some sort of satisfaction. The medieval guilds controlled the various trades, making sure that apprentices were properly trained and ensured a high standard of work. The working conditions, wages and welfare of the members was controlled by the guilds, creating a closed-shop monopoly that it was difficult to beat, so people would have little choice but to join their guild. The fellowship was eventually granted a Royal Charter by King James 1st in September 1605, after existing for centuries as a mystery or fellowship. The guild now had the power to control all the various aspects of the gardener's work:

> 'The trade, crafte or misterie of gardening, planting, grafting, setting, sowing, cutting, arboring, rocking, mounting, covering, fencing and removing of plants, herbes, seedes, fruites, trees, stocks, setts...'

These were the same horticultural tasks that would have been expected of any good medieval gardener.

Whatever their training, a gardener's work was varied. In 1412–13, two men were paid 8d to cut down trees in the garden. For the onerous task of rooting out the brambles in the garden and in the meadow next to the great park, one man was paid 4s. 4d. Winter work could include general maintenance such as making a hedge and ditch in the garden, cost 8s.7d.

Most estates paid expenses and received rents and other dues four times a year. Payment were set for each term, or quarter, and were payable on the Quarter Days. The Quarter Days vary over time and in different regions of the country. Higham Ferrers accounts, 1313–14, give these days as:

Our Lord's Nativity, 25 December; Easter; St John Baptist, 24 June; and Michaelmas, 29 September. Hock Day or Hockeday, the second Tuesday after Easter, was an old English festival and an alternative to Easter as one of the Term Days. As a non-floating alternative to Easter, Annunciation Day on 25 March became more common. Gardeners with regular employment were often paid quarterly in cash and kind which could include rations of peas and grains. As with many other positions, a gardener often received clothing as part of his wages. The cellarer at Norwich often recorded payments for the gardeners' protective leggings, shoes and tunics. The gardener at Winchester College received an ell of linen cloth for his apron in 1407/8. At Battle Abbey in 1420/21, Robert Nore the gardener was paid 5 shillings for his livery and for his salary, besides 3s. 4d paid by the lord. Whilst Thomas Underclif, the cellarer's gardener, was paid yearly the sum of 6s 8d, whilst an extra 5s was allowed for his livery during 1465–66. And for some, payment was not always prompt. In 1478–79, John Jay the gardener was paid for a year and a half up to Michaelmas, his wages being 10s with another 6s 8d for his robe.

The more skillful work could be much better paid. A shilling a day was being paid in wages for the keeper of the king's vines at Windsor in 1359, over double what most gardeners were earning at the time.

A labourer's daily wages usually included their food and drink. The drink was usually in the form of low alcohol small ale or cider. The accounts for Battle Abbey in 1369/70, noted that for scything all the meadows, and for spreading, lifting and gathering the hay, the cost was 65s, more than usual, and this was because the work was carried out without bread, ale or cheese being given in part-payment to the workmen. A garden labourer's work was physically tough and poorly paid. A practical gardener's wages have always been notoriously low and have never been good when compared to other trades.

The following late fourteenth century complaint is from a French conversation book, *La Manière de Langage*, that had been translated into English at Bury St Edmunds. It may be made up, but it sounds true enough:

'I have grafted all the trees in my garden with the fairest grafts that I have seen for a long while, and they are beginning to put forth green; also I have dug another garden and I have carefully planted cabbages, porry, parsley and sage and other goodly herbs. And furthermore I have pulled up and cleared away from it all the nettles, brambles and wicked weeds, and I have sown it full well with many good seeds; and in it I have likewise many fair trees bearing divers fruits, such as apples, pears, plums, cherries and nuts, and everywhere have I very well looked after them, yet all I have earned this week is 3d and my expenses; but last week I earned as much again and I was very quick about it.

You can imagine the person he is speaking to nodding in agreement as he replies, 'One must earn what one can today!'

It sounds that this gardener was usually employed as casual labour, and that his pay was poor, no matter how skilled he was.

It was often a part of the wages to be fed and watered for your day's work, as recorded at Battle Abbey in 1369–1370:

'For scything all the meadows and for spreading, lifting and gathering the hay this year, 65s. and so much because without bread, ale and cheese.'

Weeding was an important part of a gardener's work but pay was poor. (Getty image)

CHAPTER 10

The Gardener's Tools and Equipment

The tools of the medieval gardener were virtually unchanged since the Roman period. There may not have been the selection that is available today, yet they have survived in use into the modern period, and most would remain unchanged until the Industrial Revolution. We have extensive expense records that record the cost of buying or repairing tools, audits of the tools that were kept on site, while archaeology has found the remains of tools. Many wealthy laymen owned lavishly illustrated Books of Hours, which show the daily prayers that were to be said, and Psalters that contain the Psalms. Both books usually included illustrations of the monthly labours in their calendars. Other pictorial guides include tapestries, stained glass windows, and some of the misericord seats in the larger churches show workers with garden and agricultural tools.

During the twelfth century, Alexander Neckham gave a list of tools in his *De Utensilibus*, where he said that the gardener should have a fork, a wide blade, a spade or shovel, a knife, a seed basket for seed-time, a wheelbarrow, a basket, a pannier and a trap for sparrow-hawks. He will need a two-edged axe to remove thorns, brambles, briars, prickles and other unwanted shoots and he should have a supply of rushes and wood to mend hedges, and timbers, palings and stakes or hedging hurdles. He must have a knife hanging from his belt to graft trees, and mattocks for uprooting nettles, vetch, darnel, thistles, sterile oats and similar weeds, and a hoe for tares.

Abingdon Abbey has a similar list of the equipment that it owned that dates to c.1189. There were four ladders, an axe, a saw, three augers for boring holes, two sieves, a rope, two iron forks for Autumn which were probably pitchforks, a seed-basket, a bushel measure, a mallet, two pairs of shears, a scythe, two sickles, three spades, three shovels and two rakes for gathering moss. John Garlande adds pruning hooks and traps for wolves and mice.

Any modern gardener will recognise the tools in these lists. There are notable absences. There are no digging forks, nor one-handed trowels, nor weeding forks. The most likely reason that digging forks were not used is because the tempering of the metal was not good enough to prevent the tines from bending. Digging forks do not become common until the Industrial Revolution.

Spade

The early spade had a wooden handle and blade cut from one plank of wood that was edged with an iron shoe. The iron protected the wooden head from damage and could be sharpened, making the spade easier to use. The top of the spade handle is most often shown as a D or T shape.

The shape of the blade also varied and could be square or heart shaped. The blade of the spade could have one or two sides for the foot to push it into the soil. One advantage of having only one side to place the foot is that a spade can easily be made from a narrow plank and that two spades could be cut, head to handle, from a slightly longer plank, which saves wasting a lot of wood. Many examples of spades have been found by archaeologists, dating from the Roman period onwards. The length of the handle and blade is approximately one metre. The metal blade tip may add up to 10cm to the total length.

Ludlow misericorde showing a spade with only one edge for the foot.

The spade was useful as a weapon too; the Bayeux Tapestry shows two men fighting each other with spades during the construction of a motte and bailey castle.

The remains of the spades that have been found often comprise just the head with the corroded metal still attached. The iron expands and distorts over the centuries and this has led to many people regarding wooden spades as heavy and inefficient tools. Some historians have suggested that spades were made of wood simply because metal was expensive, but the price of a mattock was often only a penny more than a spade. This is not such a huge difference in price. The wooden spade, although cheap and quick to produce, would never be as efficient as a spade with a metal blade. One reason that spades with metal blades took so long to become commonly used is because the metal could not easily be tempered hard enough to prevent a metal spade blade from bending. Another reason that wooden spades continued in use is more practical: the gardeners are usually shown working in bare feet or thin-soled shoes. Such a gardener digging with a metal spade would be injured within minutes; by the Victorian period gardeners protected their leather soled boots by strapping a 'digging iron' to the sole of the foot they used to push down the spade to prevent the top edge of the metal spade cutting through their expensive leather-soled boots. There are a few continental medieval pictures that show metal blade spades, but it is not until the Industrial Revolution that steel was reliably tempered hard enough for the metal blade spade to become ubiquitous, although the wooden spade continued in use until the early twentieth century.

Mattock

The mattock is a spade with its head at right angles to the shaft. It is used in similar fashion to a pickaxe. This saves much back bending. A mattock is especially useful for clearing and digging soil. One wood cut shows the gardener using his mattock to plant with, in much the same way as we now use a trowel.

The mattock can also be used as a pull-hoe. Mattocks are shown in different sizes, which begs the question, at what point does a mattock become a hoe?

Strabo called the mattock the tooth of Saturn, the god who ate his own children. In his poem, Strabo said that he used his mattock to clear the noxious weeds from the soil.

Mattock.

Spud

The spud was another tool that had been used by the Romans. It had a long handle with a rounded head on the end that could be used in a similar fashion as a hoe or as a lever to lift large pieces of stone out of the soil. The spud was certainly in use during the medieval period, but it is not shown in pictures as often as either the spade or the mattock.

Shovels

The shovel was made in much the same way as a wooden spade, being cut from one piece of wood. Some pictures show the shovel as being made entirely of wood. Others show a thin metal plate to protect the edge. Shovels tended to be used for moving soil and manure, but the narrow-bladed metal-edged shovel could have also been used for digging. A shovel cost the cellarer at Norwich 3d in 1483.

Claw

Crescenzi said that you should carry out the weeding with an iron tool shaped like a hand. He may have meant a mattock, the arm being the handle and then bending the fingers at ninety degrees. The Romans had used the *bicornis*, a two pronged tool similar to a modern cultivator. The tool is shown as a long handled tool in many medieval

Author's replica of Crescenzi's claw.

Wooden shovels.

illustrations, but in a late copy of Crescenzi's book, a gardener is shown holding one of these tools. With its short handle and two bent prongs, it does appear similar to a hand.

Rake

Several illuminations show gardeners with a wooden rake for levelling the soil and creating a fine tilth. Roman rakes have survived that use iron nails for the tines, but the rake was usually made completely of wood.

Strabo used a rake to break his soil to a fine tilth, whilst the Norwich Cathedral accounts of 1484 show that moss was raked from the grass of the cloister garth. This is one job where a rake with metal tines would be much better.

Wooden rake with wooden tines.

Knives

Knives were of various sizes with blade shapes suited for different uses such as pruning and grafting. The blades that have been found by archaeology are usually a smaller version of the curved billhook. The Romans had used pruning

Pruning knife.

knives and they continued to be the main tool for the job until secateurs were introduced in the nineteenth century and became so popular that pruning knives are rarely used nowadays.

The medieval pruning knife varied in size but usually had a blade with an in-facing curve at the tip to help cut through the wood. You could think of the pruning knife as a miniature billhook. The gardeners are sometimes shown with a pruning knife tucked into the belt at the waist, ready for use. At Norwich, two shillings was regularly paid to buy knives for cutting the cabbages.

Billhook

Billhooks have been found by archaeology that date back to the Roman period. Accurate dating is difficult as shapes and sizes vary, but more by the geographical area rather than by the time period. Billhooks usually have a short handle but the blade can be curved similar to the pruning knife or it can be rectangular. Sometimes there is another blade on the back. The billhook could be used for pruning larger branches, coppicing and hedge laying. Long handled hooks, known as slashers, were used for cutting hedges.

Billhooks have many blade patterns.

Weeding Hook

This has a wooden handle about a metre long, with a small sharp-edged hook on the end. To use the weeding hook, you also need a forked stick of the same length. You hold the hook against the weed just above ground level. The hook is placed behind the weed, just above or below the forked stick and pulled towards you, cutting the weed. This would be an easier and quicker method to prevent thistles and docks from seeding than trying to dig them out during the growing season.

Weeding hook. (Guildhall Museum, Leicester)

Mallets

Large wooden mallets, sometimes known as beetles, were used to break up the large clods of soil that were too hard to be made finer using rakes, as shown in the *Luttrel Psalter* and other medieval manuscripts, where workers are breaking large clods of soil in the fields. Mallets were also used to beat new-laid turves into the ground.

Wooden mallet.

Saws

Saws were made in various sizes for pruning and cutting timber. The smaller hand pruning saw, similar to those still used in modern use, is shown in illuminations; whilst the larger saws tend to have a frame of wood, with an adjustable cord to put tension on the blade, which is usually narrower than the blade of a hand saw. Battle Abbey records paying 10d for a saw in 1278–1279, but by 1387/88 the cost of a saw for Norwich had increased to 1s 2d.

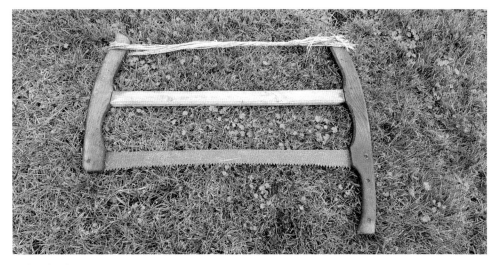

Medieval style saw.

Scythe

Scythes were expensive tools because of the amount of metal in the blade and the time taken to forge it to a suitable thinness. The medieval scythe blade had a socket that attached to a straight handle with two handles. The modern English bent handle, known as the snathe, is thought to have been developed later as a means to get the blade to lay flat on the ground so that it is easier to cut lawns with an even finish.

The resulting scythe is heavier and more difficult to use than a bent snathe. The blades were sharpened by gently thinning along the edge using a peening hammer on a field anvil. The burr was taken off using a strickle which is a piece of wood coated with animal grease and sand. It was often carried in a cow horn worn on the mower's belt.

An illustration in one copy of Crescenzi's book shows a man scything. Tucked into the back of his belt is a ground anvil and a multi-purpose hammer. Scythes were used mostly to cut hay, which being a valuable commodity, was made from any available grass. Even in modern Europe roadside verges are often cut for hay. The centre of cloisters often had a lawn, which was considered to be restful on the mind. These would probably be cut regularly. Scythes can produce a very fine surface in the hands of an experienced worker. In 1278–1279 the monks at Battle Abbey recorded, 'for one scythe 12d' and the cellarer at Norwich paid a penny halfpenny for a scythe to be repaired in 1483.

Medieval scythe with the strickle or whet stone attached to the handle.

Gardener using a peening hammer to sharpen a scythe blade.

Shears

The shears are what would now be commonly called sheep shears. The blades and handles are all in one piece, with a loop at one end that provides the spring to make them easy to operate.

They have been in use since at least the Roman period. One of the oldest pair of shears in Britain was found at Flag Fen near Peterborough. They had been deposited in the water, along with their wooden container, as an offering.

Shears were used by many different trades before the invention of scissors, including tailors, barbers and the fletchers. Gardeners can use them to trim the grass of turf seats and grass areas that scythes could not get at, to trim the estrades (topiary), for dead-heading and for cutting back herbaceous plants.

For a good cut the blades must be gripped where the blades cross.

Metal shears were useful for clipping herbs and small shrubs.

Planting Dibber

John the Gardener is probably the first British person to mention the dibber when he says of saffron, 'Plant him deep with a dibber.' Today we would instantly think of a broken fork or spade handle that has been sharpened to make a dibber. Yet it is not so obvious what the actual shape of the dibber that John mentions is. It could have been a simple piece of wood. John said that it should have a blunted end and this would avoid the risk of air pocket at the base of the hole when you

Dibber made from a piece of coppiced hazel.

dropped the seeds or plants in. The earliest known picture of a dibber is from the Tudor period and is shown in Thomas Hill's *Gardeners' Labyrinth*, where a man is planting with a dibber with a T-shaped handle. Close by another dibber lies on the ground. It has two small prongs on the end. It is possible that John used a similar dibber; we can never be certain.

Wheelbarrow

Early wheelbarrows had no sides, just a piece of wood or a wattle panel behind the wheel to hold the load in place. Sometimes the loads are carried in a basket. The body of the barrow is usually shown as being nearly flat but dipped in the middle before rising towards the handles. From the evidence we have, the Romans did not use wheelbarrows, but they did use handcarts. Dung was often carried by the gardening slaves on their backs in large baskets, a practice that continued into the medieval period. Some suggest that the wheelbarrow came from China. The Chinese wheelbarrow has the wheel in the centre of the body, which greatly reduces the size of the load to be carried.

Reconstruction of a medieval wheelbarrow.

A GUIDE TO MEDIEVAL GARDENS

Illustrations of medieval building sites show men carrying loads on a stretcher, not dissimilar to a wheelbarrow with two sets of handles but with no wheel. It is not beyond reason that somebody realised that replacing a man with a wheel would reduce labour costs. The verdict is still open.

The earliest image of a wheelbarrow in England is in Matthew Paris' manuscript, *The Life of St Alban*. Wheelbarrows are shown in manuscripts and misericorde seat carvings. The Battle Abbey accounts of 1440–41 record that 6d was paid to have two wheelbarrows made, and another 9d was paid for a wheel. Larger hand barrows had been used by the Romans. They are also recorded in medieval documents.

Baskets

Baskets were cheap to make and not so prone to breakage as pottery. They have been used as plant containers since the Roman period and are shown for the same use in the medieval period. The plant and basket can be dropped into a hole and the hole backfilled. The gaps in the basket will allow roots to grow into the surrounding soil and eventually the basket will rot away with no damage to the plant's root system.

Baskets were used to carry plants and to harvest crops, especially the grapes.

The large baskets carried on the back were often used to move manure as it was often easier to walk across uneven ground than to use a wheelbarrow.

Another use of baskets was to measure quantity, such as with bushel baskets, a bushel being a common measurement for grain and seeds. Crescenzi continued to recommend Roman advice of growing willow on any wet parts of your land for making baskets.

Large baskets were used for harvesting crops and carrying manure.

Water Pots

There were several ways to water plants, but the simplest direct method was the water pot. These simple pots have been found at many medieval sites during excavations and can be seen at museums such as the British Museum and the Museum of London. It is a small earthenware pot with a flat bottom that is full of small holes, similar to a modern watering can rose. The neck of the pot is pulled upwards and has single small hole in the top.

The pot is immersed in water. When the bubbling stops it is full. The gardener turns their hand palm upwards and holds the pot between the first two fingers and places the thumb over the top hole. The pot must be kept level, or the water will begin to leak out of the holes in the bottom. To water the plants, you simply lift your thumb and replace it to stop the water flow. Some of the pots that have been found are quite large, so there is often a finger-ring on the neck to help make it easier to hold securely when you lift it. You could also make cheap watering pots from gourds. In 1464–65 Battle Abbey paid 2d for earthen pots for watering the plants in both the cellarer's garden and the same again for the kitchen garden. They must have been in common use as the British Museum has an embossed leather knife scabbard that shows a water pot releasing its water.

Later still in the late fifteenth century, the watering pot was moulded onto the top edge of a jug, which is the forerunner of the modern watering can. Watering pots and jugs have splashes of glazing for decoration. They are rarely fully glazed as the water never has time to be lost through seepage.

Above left: *Gardener using a watering pot.*

Above right: *Pottery and gourd watering pots and a watering jug.*

Flowerpots

Potted plants were grown in gardens and houses. Scenes of the Annunciation usually include a pot of white lilies, while the pots can show a great variety of materials and shapes. Most of the flowerpots that have been found are plain earthenware, but illustrations often show finely made *maiolica* pots decorated with a blue and white glaze. A similar pot, dating to the mid-fifteenth century, known as the Basil Pot, can be seen at Waddesdon Manor, Buckinghamshire. Pots found at the Pope's Palace at Avignon include a goblet shaped pot with a brown external glaze, whilst another one has holes around the top edge, as if it were intended for cut flowers or bulbs.

In England, archaeologists found a Beverley-ware pot decorated with three beaked heads and with three vertical loops, which suggests that it could have been suspended on cords or chains, like a modern hanging basket. One illustration shows a very modern style pot with the drainage hole on the side, in the same way as the Roman flowerpot that was found at Fishbourne.

As is the case today, people could have planted in pots that were unfit for their original purpose. Earthenware is a soft material, so it is very easy to make drainage holes with a sharp piece of metal in any type of pot. Once broken and thrown away, who would ever realise the pot had once been used to grow plants.

Wooden window boxes filled with plants are sometimes shown in illuminated manuscripts.

Replica medieval flowerpot.

A replica of a bird-headed Beverley-ware flowerpot.

Aprons

An item of very practical use. Firstly, to protect the gardener's clothes, which in comparison to modern times were very expensive; secondly, an apron can be used to gather flowers and fruit; and thirdly, seed can be held in the apron as you are sowing as is shown in numerous pictures of the time.

Clothing was so expensive during the medieval period that it was common practice for clothing to be part of the wages. The accounts for Battle Abbey of 1420–21 show a payment to: 'Robert Nore, gardinar, for his livery 5s.'

The records of Winchester College 1407–1408 show 5d being spent on an ell of linen for the gardener's apron. The cost of the gardener's aprons at Apethorpe Hall in Northamptonshire were still being recorded in the eighteenth century.

Gloves

Gloves were bought for the gardeners by the cellarer at Norwich. The Museum of London has a thick leather mitten that may have been used by somebody laying hedges, and the *Luttrel Psalter* clearly shows agricultural workers wearing the standard five finger glove but also wearing another type made with a thumb and two fingers. This style of glove is simple to make as you don't need to sew each finger on separately and they offer enough flexibility to carry out many tasks. Mittens are even simpler to make, and although they would not be suitable for most jobs, they were used by people laying hedges until very recently. A medieval mitten of thick leather was found during excavations and is now on display in the Museum of London.

Medieval glove based on those shown in the Luttrell Psalter.

CHAPTER 11

Cultivation Techniques

Surprisingly little documentation has survived on the gardening techniques that were used throughout the medieval period. Using a combination of sources, we can trace some of the medieval horticultural methods. There are more gardening methods recorded from the Tudor period, but we can never be sure that these are a continuation from the medieval period. Many of the surviving medieval documents about growing plants were copied from the classical authors, who continue to be quoted extensively. What we will never know is the daily practical knowledge that the gardeners used which must have been passed on orally by master gardeners or within families.

The subject of maintaining medieval gardens has been largely ignored. Very little has been written on the subject in recent years and illuminations may show some details of the tools being used, but we have no idea of the degree of maintenance of medieval pleasure gardens that was expected during the period. Then as now, the maintenance of the gardens would be dependent on the amount of available labour, the tools that were used and on how and when the gardens were mostly used. Many of the landed gentry moved to their various properties around the country. Was the garden expected to be only used for a few weeks, or even a few days, every year? Did the lord only pay for a high level of maintenance prior to his return to the property and until he departed again? The maintenance could be reduced until his next visit, saving on expenses. Would a pleasure garden be made to look its best if the owner was expecting an important visitor who they wished to impress? Were there crops, fruit and vegetables to be grown and harvested for personal use? Financial accounts show that produce such as fruit, vegetables and hay from the orchards was being sold.

Can we discover more about how the plants were tended at the time? How were the vines tied? How do you test your soil? Which plants were being grown, and what would you do with them?

Strabo the monk said that joy comes from gardening. He didn't beat about the bush about the effort that you needed to put into your garden for it to be productive, and that to get good results, you must be prepared to put in a lot of hard work and get your hands dirty.

Another source of garden information is the *Ménagier de Paris*, which is a handbook written in the fourteenth century by an elderly Frenchman for his younger wife. There is no particular order to his writing and he sometimes repeats himself, maybe because he wrote things down as he thought of them and did not intend to edit the book for other readers, it being intended only for his wife. He gives advice on how to run the household. This includes the tending of horses and hawks, the planning of menus, including suitable recipes. There are instructions on how to deal with servants, with a warning not to pay workmen at lunch time on Friday or they will not return that afternoon, as true today as then! There is a section on gardening where the *Ménagier* makes no reference to the classical authorities on gardening as he is not trying to impress an elite literate group but aims simply to help his spouse. He offers sound horticultural advice as it was probably generally practised at that time. His wife is instructed on the sowing of seed, how to water properly, and the best way to harvest the crops. There is even advice on how to deal with ants and caterpillars.

Digging and Soil Preparation

Walafrid Strabo stresses the point that he is writing from personal experience, common knowledge and from reading old books. He begins with the encouraging words that no matter what type of soil your garden has, there will always be something that will grow well. It doesn't matter if the soil in your garden is sandy or gravel, whether the site is high on a hill, or down in the plain, your garden will produce a good harvest if you are careful to choose plants that are suited to the conditions. You must be prepared to work outdoors, whatever the weather and harden your hands with the physical work of digging and carrying manure, or your efforts will be in vain. Strabo dug out the nettles, they came up again, so once more, he had to dig them out. He made raised beds edged with planks to stop the rain washing away the soil. He raked the soil to a fine tilth and worked in manure before sowing seeds or transplanting herbs from elsewhere while, as he said, they appeared to be dead, meaning that the plants were dormant. Even today, most gardeners would prefer to move plants before they actively begin to grow. Very soon Strabo's garden was green with healthy plants. Crescenzi, who copied much of his material from the Romans, adds more ideas. He suggests improving a clay soil with manure or ashes and sandy soil with manure, but he recommends that the manure must always be added a little at a time. He used raised beds with channels around them so water could be allowed to the beds and the sides could be opened to water the plants. this method is till used in rural area of mainland Europe. Some medieval sources say that the fields should be ploughed three times. This would allow the weeds seeds to germinate and then be destroyed by the next ploughing. The *Liber Niger*, the Black Book of Kettering Manor in Northamptonshire, states that even more work was required and that you should plough your land three times in winter, three times in spring and once in summer. Over time this would reduce the weed seed reserve in the soil, making it easier to keep weeds under control as time goes by. Some of the more persistent perennial weed roots may be destroyed by regular ploughing or digging. This method could be used in the decorative and productive gardens, but digging with a spade or mattock, instead of ploughing, although at Norwich cathedral they spent 1s to have the garden ploughed. John Gardener said that you should dig the soil but gives no explanation as to how this should be done.

It could be that the Roman methods of trenching had continued to be passed on through the ages or reintroduced by monks, but we cannot be certain. It is likely that garden soil would also be dug twice. The first dig would be in autumn, exposing pests and their eggs to the birds. Annual weeds could be turned into the soil, adding their nutrients as they rotted. Over the winter months, heavy soils would be broken down by wind, rain and frost. A second dig in the late winter or early spring would ensure that the soil has been well mixed, or well-stirred as John Gardener says, with less chance of root scorch from manure. Wooden mallets were used to break any large lumps of soil, then a rake would be used to create a fine tilth suitable for sowing seeds. Sieves are recorded as part of the gardener's equipment, so may have been used to help create a fine tilth for seed sowing in small gardens and probably for separating seeds from seed cases to save them for later use.

A medieval gardener prepares the soil for planting.

Lawns

The lawns that are mostly seen in medieval illustrations and the *Mille-Fleurs* tapestries are the colourful flowery meads, where the grass is brightly bedecked with blooming flowers. The famous *Lady and the Unicorn* tapestries at the Cluny Museum in Paris are typical with their depiction of the flowering turf. Yet art is not entirely honest: the flowers would certainly not have all been in full bloom at the same time. It is very much a delightful illusion that is virtually impossible to replicate in a real garden.

Not all the lawns were maintained as flowery meads, because the monks at Norwich cathedral paid some labourers 6d to rake the grass in the cloister garth to remove the moss. At that time, green was considered to be a meditative colour, so a green sward was thought to have a calming effect on the monks.

Preparing the soil for a lawn is still a laborious process. We are lucky to have a first-hand account from the medieval period from Albertus Magnus, who wrote detailed instructions on how you should prepare the soil to make a lawn. The land should first be ploughed and then drenched with boiling water to kill any remaining weed roots and seeds in the soil. This process would work equally as well for preparing flower beds.

The turves for the lawn could be cut from nearby meadows, probably to include colourful wildflowers. So far, the cultivation is like modern methods, other than we would use herbicides rather than hot water to kill the weeds. It was at this point that horticultural practice was very much different from what we would do today. Rather than carefully laying the turf without stepping on it, the medieval gardeners beat the turf into the soil using wooden mallets until the blades of grass barely showed above the surface of the soil. We are told that this will produce a closely growing turf that will resemble velvet. This may sound a rather harsh treatment to modern horticulturalists, but for

Tools to help clean up the grass trimmings after scything.

centuries the main tool for cutting grass was the scythe. Modern man carefully tends the lawn with thorough soil preparation, feeding, irrigation, scarifying, aeration and top-dressing, which can result in three cuts of the lawn per week in good growing weather. Compacting the topsoil with mallets will restrict the growth of the grass so that it will not need cutting too often, which is ideal if you only have a scythe to keep the grass short. We do not know how often lawns would have been cut, only that it was recommended that the grass in orchards should be cut twice a year. The grass tops of turf seats could be cut easily with hand shears as necessary. Short clippings were probably cleared up using a besom broom or a rake. A hayfork could be used for the longer grass in an orchard.

Fertiliser

The value of fertilising the soil was mentioned by Roman writers who said that dove dung was one of the best manures to use, and it was readily available as doves were an important source of meat and income for a manor. Strabo mentioned manuring and says that by adding baskets of manure to even dry soil, you will ensure a good harvest. John Gardener said that the soil should be dug and stirred well.

In crop fields, the animals could be put out to graze and they would provide manure at the same time. Gardeners could collect manure from the animal's winter quarters, with the dung of cattle and sheep being better than that of horses. There was dung from the dovecote, and not forgetting there was a good supply of human excrement when the privies were emptied.

For garden use, the water used for boiling beans was considered to be a useful fertiliser.

The Influence of the Stars

There was a strong belief in astrology during the middle ages that derived from antiquity. The sun, moon, planets, stars and other astronomical phenomena were thought to influence life on earth. Ancient civilisations may have noticed that the position of certain stars coincided with the planting time for certain crops, but the idea came into being that the moon and stars were not just markers of time, but were actually responsible as causes of the growth.

At some time in antiquity the relationship between the moon and the tides of the seas had been noted. From this it was inferred that the moon was also important for the sowing of seeds and for harvesting. For leafy crops that grow above ground the moon should be waxing. For root vegetables it should be on the wane. For crops that were to be eaten immediately, harvest at the waxing moon. Crops that were to be stored dry should be picked at the waning or new moon. Unfortunately, the ancient writers do not always agree with each other about the specifics of lunar phases, which leave some of their observations in doubt. It would seem that a good gardener of the medieval period would need to be well educated in astronomy to make good use of the following extract from the Pocklington manuscript in the British Library:

'When the moon is in Taurus it is good to plant trees from pips, and when it is in Cancer, Leo or in Libra, then it is good to work on trees that are newly sprung: and when the moon is in the Virgin it is a good time to sow all manner of thing...'

The church, by default, provided a calendar for those who could not read or write, because the saints' days and other Christian festivals marked the passing year. Many writers name the saints' days and other important church feast days as a method of knowing when to plant or carry out horticultural practices such as pruning, sowing and harvesting:

'And know well that every tree that is planted and set in the earth on the feast of Saint Lambarte [September 17] shall not perish that year.'

Possibly depicts a decorated statue of Mary or a woman celebrating the sowing of the crops. (Ripple church)

A GUIDE TO MEDIEVAL GARDENS

The church was involved with the growing of food. April 25th was the major Rogation Day of the Catholic church. It replaced the pagan Roman feast of Robigalia, when a puppy dog was sacrificed to Robigus to ensure wheat crops were protected from the disease known as rust. The Church celebrations often involved processions that could include the carrying of a statue of the Virgin Mary into the fields to ensure fertility.

There would be a celebration at the end of the harvest to thank God for his benevolence.

Some gardening ideas recorded from the medieval period may involve a lot of wishful thinking, although to be fair, many of these ideas were being repeated from Roman sources, and the Romans had some odd ideas about gardening. Although there is mention that the gardeners of Emperor Tiberius used an early form of greenhouse on a cart to grow cucumbers out of season, there are no records of similar practices during the medieval period, except for a reference to Albertus Magnus surprising his visitors in Cologne by showing them plants in flower and fruit that he grew in the shelter of the cloisters. But the care of tender plants that would be killed by cold weather was well understood. Violets were grown especially for their scent and colour, but the best ones were tender, so you would need to protect them over winter by putting the pots in the cellar. Once the worse of the cold weather was over, the plants would need to be gently hardened-off by only putting them out on warm days and then putting them back under cover at night to prevent them being killed by the cold. You had to remember not move the plants suddenly from cold to warmth, nor from damp to cold. If you had kept them in a cool, damp cellar for a long time and then suddenly put them in a dry place, they would die, and vice versa. In Paris, Armenian violets did not need cover nor shelter from cold weather and could be grown outdoors all year. However, they would not flower until their second year, so gardeners who had already been growing them for a year could dig them up and sell them or replant them elsewhere in their garden and they would flower that same year. The *Ménagier de Paris* told his young wife that is best to plant in rainy weather, but not too wet. In 1465/66 the cellarer at Norwich complained that the garden had not made so much money as usual because flood water had drowned the seeds.

Seeds would be needed to be saved for the next year's crops and should be kept in wooden boxes or bags to protect them from vermin. The heavy seed heads of onions were propped off the ground using forked sticks of ash wood.

Seeds were sown broadcast both in the fields and in gardens; the idea of sowing seeds in straight lines would not take hold until much later. In the garden, seeds would be scattered on the soil and then raked in to cover them, so it was best to sow small seeds in dry weather so the seeds wouldn't stick to the rake. It was well understood that wet soil could be ridged so that it drained well before planting or sowing. It was advised to change your seed every Michaelmas, as seed from other men's land would re-invigorate your crops. Seed was often bought in from elsewhere as there are many

Gardeners planting using their hands as their employer points to where the plants should be placed. Note the aprons and baskets used to hold plants. In the background gardeners train plants to the tunnel arbour that leads off from the gloriette. (Alarmy picture)

records of the time that mention itinerant traders selling seeds. It was considered a good idea to bring fresh vigour to your crops by using seed from elsewhere.

Planting and grafting were ideally carried out during damp weather. The best times of the day for planting were in the evening or early in the morning before the sun became hot, and preferably when the moon was waning.

One medieval gardening tip, known as 'puddling-in', is still used today during dry weather. Dig the planting hole, then carefully pour water into the hole and allow the water to soak away before placing the plant, but do not do this when the soil is already wet.

Watering Plants

The *Ménagier* says you should only water the stem and the earth around the plant, not the leaves. With wisdom that is still followed today, he advised that you should not water plants when the sun is hot, but in the morning or evening when the temperature is cooler. Strabo collected water in a bucket and carefully watered his seeds through his fingers. Watering could be carried out with a bucket and a pot.

You could water plants more gently by using a pot that has had a small hole drilled in the bottom. Prop the pot up on a stick, push a piece of straw into the hole and place the other end close to the stem of the plant so the water can seep down and keep the soil moist. A piece of cloth could be placed in the mouth of the jug and the other end placed on the soil near the plant.

Watering by capillary action using a piece of cloth.

Weeding

Plants need space to grow to full size. Thinning vegetable seedlings to allow space for crops to fully develop was recommended in gardens, if not fields. But weeds were the main problem. Removing unwanted plants from gardens and fields is one of the essential tasks of gardeners and farmers. It was understood that weeds would take the nourishment and water that your crops needed. We know from records that women could be paid 2½d a day for weeding and that children were paid even less for weeding field crops, but neither Walafrid Strabo nor John Gardener tell us how the weeds were removed; it was something that everybody would know! If the soil had been prepared correctly the weeds can easily be removed by pulling them out by hand in small gardens. In larger areas a mattock could be used in the same way as a modern hoe. We cannot even be certain of the standards of maintenance that were expected at the time. Which plants did medieval gardeners regard as weeds? Strabo certainly considered nettles as weeds because he dug them out with his mattock, and he had to do this more than once, as any gardener today would be aware. The pretty yellow corn marigold, *Chrysanthemum segetum*, known as golds, and grown as a decorative plant by modern gardeners, was a major weed of cornfields during the medieval period. Unlike corncockle, it is not toxic, but it is slow to dry out and could cause the straw to rot.

It must have been considered a major problem because Henry II issued a decree against it; the earliest known English order to destroy a specific weed. The Battle Abbey accounts for 1478–79 show that 2s was paid for scything thistles before ploughing for oats; but timing was important as it was recommended that thistles should not be cut down before St John's Day, otherwise you would have two or three extra thistles growing for each one that you had cut down. In a vegetable garden some weeds and plants that we now consider to be weeds may have been tolerated because they are edible or had other uses, such as avens, *Geum urbanum*, and groundsel, *Senecio vulgaris*, which were being deliberately sown and cultivated by John Gardener, but this this would probably not be the case in a decorative garden. Many people's expectations of modern gardens are such that any plant which spoils a decorative effect must be removed. I found that any plants that are usually considered to be weeds can only be left growing in a modern medieval garden if it is explained to visitors why they are being allowed to grow. Many of the common herbs are free seeding and can become a problem as bad as the weeds themselves if they are not controlled, but if we ruthlessly weed out the self-seeding herbs too thoroughly the garden may become soulless. Decorative plants that have self-seeded outside their original allocated space usually cause no harm and many gardeners will allow them to bloom in peace. The anonymous poem, *The Assembly of Ladies*, c.1450, suggests that medieval gardeners were not always over-zealous when it came to weeding:

> 'The poor pansies were not dislodged there,
> No, no, God knows, they were growing everywhere.'

Corn marigold, Chrysanthemum segetum. Henry II decreed that it should be destroyed if found growing in the crops.

Heartsease could be found growing everywhere.

Harvesting

After all the work involved with soil, preparation, sowing, weeding, watering, scaring off the birds and killing the other pests and maybe blessings from the priest, the final reward would be harvesting your crops.

Care was needed when removing the leaves from the cut-and-come again vegetables. The leaves must not be cut from cabbage, parsley, or other green-leaf vegetables when the sun was hot because the heat of the sun would harden and burn the wound, so that the plant wouldn't grow again from that point. The picking of ripe fruit from trees was a dangerous affair. There were no dwarfing rootstocks to restrict the height of medieval apple and pear trees, which would grow much taller than the modern trees to be found even in a commercial orchard. Illustrations show men standing on branches in the trees having climbed tapered ladders that are wider at the base so they will be more stable. Sometimes baskets hang on sticks suspended from the tree branches so that it is easy to collect the fruit. A few pictures show people who are scrumping, taking the fruit that belongs to somebody else; they are usually stealing cherries. Late ripening apples and the very hard Warden pears could be kept over winter in dark, frost free sheds. Damaged fruit would be cooked as soon as possible. Peas and beans were usually cut down with scythes once the stems and seeds had dried out. Peas

Winter savoury was reputed to prevent flatulence.

were threshed in the same way as corn, the stems were not wasted as they were fed to animals. The beans were probably threshed to remove them from the dried pods. Many herbals and medical books refer to beans being a major source of flatulence. Some books recommend cooking and then changing the water to reduce this; others suggest cooking with herbs such as winter savoury as a way to solve the problem.

Pruning

Pruning is an essential horticultural practice to encourage plants to grow in the way that you would like them to. It helps rejuvenate old plants, promotes flowering and fruiting and can be used to shape plants. How much a medieval gardener understood about encouraging fruiting we aren't certain.

For small shrubs a pruning knife would be adequate. For thicker wood, such as when coppicing willow and hazel, a billhook would be used. A saw could be used when the wood was too thick to use a billhook. For rural hedges a slasher – a billhook with a curved blade on a long handle – could be used. It can leave a reasonable face to a hedge, but it is difficult to produce a smooth finish.

For the topiary estrades it is more likely that a hook or shears would be the best tools. Gardeners could use shears or knives to trim or harvest soft plant woody material or herbaceous plants. Another tool that could be used for this purpose is a small sickle.

Grafting

Grafting is a method used to join the vigorous roots of one plant to the top growth, known as the scion, of another slower growing plant. It is an ancient technique known to the ancient Greeks and the Romans. During the medieval period grafting is shown in many pictures, and several manuscripts describe how to graft fruit trees, and it may have been used for vines and roses. Apple and pear trees could be grafted from September until April. Apple scions being grafted onto an apple tree rootstock and pears onto a hawthorn.

John Gardener said that first the rootstock is cut back using a saw, so this is quite a thick branch that he is describing. The saw blades were probably quite coarse, as we are told to smooth the cut with a knife. This will help to reduce the risk of disease and die-back. The graft scion, the tree that you want, is cut from between the old and new growth; juvenile wood will take and grow more readily than old wood. A wedge is driven into the stock to open a place for the scion, which must be placed in the split so that the bark, or rind, as John refers to it, is in line with the bark of the stock plant, otherwise the graft will not take because the sap will not be flowing into it. Withdraw the wedge and seal the area with clay covered with moss to keep out the rain, binding the graft with a strip of hazel bark. The grafting method that he gives was used for centuries afterwards, but today the graft will be bound with biodegradable plastic.

John explains how to produce more vines using cuttings. They should when there is a warmer westerly wind, not when there is a cold easterly wind. Cut a piece of vine stem with three buds and then insert it in the ground with one bud above the soil level. This is still a good way to make vine cuttings. We are advised to spread a plentiful amount of dung in the planting hole and as a mulch on the surface.

Rosemary Cuttings

The *Ménagier de Paris* said that it was a well-known fact to gardeners that rosemary seeds were difficult to germinate in the cold climate of northern France. If you wanted to propagate rosemary it was better to use slips, or cuttings as many people would refer to them now. He said that you should pick a sprig of rosemary and strip it of all its leaves from top to bottom and plant it in the soil, saying that it would soon grow. Modern gardeners would do something similar, but they would leave some of the upper leaves on the cutting. If you wanted to send cuttings of rosemary for planting some distance away, The *Ménagier* said that you should wrap the cuttings in a waxed cloth, sew up the cloth and then smear the outside of the cloth with honey and finally powder it with wheat flour, presumably to make it easier to handle. You could then send the package wherever you liked. Cuttings soon dry out, so the honey-sealed package could be used much as we would use a plastic bag today to prevent the cuttings losing their moisture.

Tying Plants

The tying of plants to supports is a much-used horticultural technique. Today we use string, but during the medieval period string would be expensive as it involves much labour to grow plant material, extract the fibres and then to spin them into thread using a drop spindle or a great wheel. Roses and vines would require tying onto the tunnel arbours, and vines would need tying onto their posts or frames in the vineyards. Even for a short tunnel arbour this would require a lot of string, but to tie in the vines of a vineyard using string would be much too expensive. Crescenzi said that rushes could be collected and dried as vine ties. He also says that willow withies could be used to tie plants in place, a practice that is still used today in Italy.

Fresh willow withies, or they may be soaked in water if dry, are put behind the support and the plant, crossed at the front and tightly twisted several times.

One end is cut off short and the other is left with 2 to 4cm surplus, which is then folded back to prevent the tie unwinding. Willow or hazel bark can be carefully stripped from the withies and used as string. The withies and the bark can be dried and stored for later use, but both will need soaking in water to become pliable again.

Plants could be tied to their supports using willow withies.

Special Practices

Some manuscripts describe special processes, most of which had been copied from Roman sources. Some would work, others are more dubious.

To Grow an Object in an Apple
An anonymous fifteenth century English writer described how to hide a pearl, a precious stone, a farthing, or something similar inside an apple so that the person who ate it would have a surprise when they bit into it, for better or worse!

> 'A method so that a pearl, a precious stone, a farthing, or any other manner of thing can be found in an apple or pear:- Take an apple or a pear after it has flowered and beginning to get larger and thrust whichever of the items you choose into the bud end of the fruit. Let it grow, and carefully mark the apple so that you remember which one it was.'

He went on to suggest that to have grapes without pips, you should remove the pith of the vine. This was done by carefully splitting the vine branches, removing the pith and then binding the branches back together. A similar process could be used to grow cherries without stones. Sadly, for all the effort involved, it does not work.

> 'To have fruit of different colours, you shall make a hole in a tree near the root, into the pith of the tree, and then put in a good dye such as Blue of Germany, so it be near full, and stop the hole well with a short pin, and wrap it well with clay, and bind it well as though it was a graft, and the fruit shall be of a blue colour. You can do the same with any vine, and all manner of colours.'

Equally unlikely to succeed was to regularly sprinkle goat's milk on the flowers of a peach tree for three days in order to produce pomegranate fruit!

To have stems of blooming roses at any time of the year, the *Ménagier* said that you should cut stems with closed buds and place them in a bottle of Beauvais earthenware. Fill the bottle with loose, dry sand and seal the top. Place the bottle in running water until you need the roses as open flowers. Open the jar and stand the stems in warm water.

For fruit that is sour, for to make it sweet, he quoted Aristotle, who said, in his *Book of Plants*, that you should dig around the tree, and add pig's dung. You can also make a hole with a wimble (a drill), to the core of the plant and pour in water mixed with honey and stop the hole again with a peg of the same tree.

If an apple tree or its fruit were rotting it was a sign that the bark of the tree was in ill health. A knife cut across the bark and would release the bad humours and could then be sealed with clay.

Pests

People have always had problems with protecting their precious plants from the depredation of animals and insects. When you had to grow your own food, pests were a much more serious menace than they are now for most modern gardeners. If the pests ate your food, you would go hungry.

Ants

The *Ménagier de Paris* said that putting oak sawdust on the anthills before rain would drive away the ants as the sawdust would retain the moisture, which the ants could not tolerate. When I went to a Lincolnshire sawmill to get some oak sawdust for demonstrations at the Prebendal Manor medieval gardens, I was asked if I wanted it to get rid of ants, so this use is still remembered by some today! Oak bark was used for tanning leather, so it is possible that the high tannin levels in oak may help drive away the ants as much as the moisture.

Slugs and Snails

Both pests are fond of eating soft growth and can quickly destroy young shoots. The easiest method to control them is to collect them by hand and the *Ménagier* included instructions on how you can then prepare snails ready for cooking! Soot and lime powder could be sprinkled around plants to deter slugs and snails.

Slugs and snails soon destroy small seedlings.

Caterpillars

The main method suggested is that you should check your cabbages regularly and remove any caterpillars that you find by hand. You could sprinkle ashes onto the leaves or use the dangerous mixture of vinegar with crushed henbane seeds.

Medieval descriptions of creepy-crawlies were rather vague, so we can't be certain of what exactly was meant by writer when he mentions worms, but caterpillars may have been intended:

> 'If worms grow in a tree, take ashes that are mixed with olive or myrrh oil, and that shall slay them.'

Slightly less pleasant, another method was to smear the tree with a mixture made with two parts of ox piss and the third part of clay.

Caterpillars are large enough to be removed by hand.

Moles

Moles have rarely been tolerated in gardens. They make a mess, but more seriously their tunnelling can kill plants by disturbing the roots. The monks at Norwich Cathedral often made payments of 1s to a molecatcher, although we have no idea how he was catching them.

It is possible that people were still using a technique, mentioned by a Roman writer, of filling a walnut shell with a mixture of sulphur and resin which you light, loosely tie the two halves of the shell together and drop it in the mole run. Thomas Hill, writing under the pen name of Didymus Montaine, repeats this method in his *Gardeners' Labyrinth* of 1594. A later book suggested employing somebody with a spear to kill the moles, which could have been used during earlier times. Another Roman method was to sink a pot into the run of mole. You could half fill the pot with water to drown the moles or add a female mole to an empty pot, to entice the males to their doom. Crushed cloves of garlic were thrown into the mole runs to persuade them to leave. Modern organic gardeners still use this method. A spade can be used to set mole traps and some people today will use a spade to flip a mole out of its run and then hit it like a cricket ball. We don't know how medieval mole catchers used their spade, but in 1434 William of Wytelbury drew blood from the chaplain, Thomas Coteler, with a mole spade, worth 6d.

Moles disturb plant roots.
(Getty Image)

Rats and Mice

One method of controlling the rodent population is to keep a few cats, but it never hurts to have a backup. John Garlande said that every house should have mousetraps, and mouse traps are mentioned in the Prologue of *The Canterbury Tales*, when Chaucer says of the prioress that: 'She would weep, if she saw a mouse caught in a trap, or if it were dead or bleeding.'

According to several herbals, rats and other vermin could be driven out of the garden by planting the bitter flavoured herb, rue, but a more efficient use of plants would be to poison the rodents using a bait of breadcrumbs mixed with the seeds or roots of hellebores, hemlock and other similarly poisonous plants. Another suggestion was to toast small pieces of cheese and make a paste, mixing in powdered aconite, *Aconitum napellus*, a well-known poisonous plant.

Shape the paste into small cakes which you can leave near the mouse holes, ideally where the mice cannot get any water to drink. If the mice have easy access to water, cut a sponge into small pieces; if the mice drink soon after swallowing the sponge, it will swell up and kill them. If you are still troubled with vermin, the following recipe would be more than enough to kill most creatures. Mix together an ounce of aconite, two ounces of powdered arsenic, a pound of fine what flour, some pigs lard and four eggs. Make this into a loaf and bake in the oven. When it has cooled, cut the loaf into strips and nail the strips to the floor where the rats and mice can find it. *Aconitum* is a very powerful poison, so it was even be used to poison wolves, foxes and wild boars. Rat catchers appear in many expense accounts of the time, but we are not told what sort of traps they were using. The *Ménagier* recommends traps made of little planks set upon sticks, which he says any good servant can make. He may be referring to simple drop traps that can be made using

The lethally poisonous Aconitum napellus was useful for killing vermin.

The Morode Altarpiece shows Joseph making a mousetrap and another outside on a window shutter. (Wiki Commons)

a plank of wood or a flat, heavy stone. The plank or stone is delicately supported by an arrangement of three sticks with some bait fixed to one of them. When the rodent nibbles the bait, the plank or stone falls, squashing the victim.

A more complicated trap that uses twisted cord to provide the power is shown in the early fifteenth century Annunciation Triptych, also known as the Merode Altarpiece.

The central panel depicts the Annunciation, whilst in the right-hand panel, Joseph is hard at work as a carpenter. A wooden trap can be seen on his workbench and there another one on a lowered shutter just outside the window. The painting shows so much detail that working copies have made of the trap and it has been proved to work effectively.

Drop trap to catch rats and mice. (Getty Image)

Wooden bird scarers were cheap and easy to make.

A manuscript, the *Paris Arsenal*, shows a rat caught in a live-trap with a door activated by a pivot. The picture shows a drop trap that was still in use centuries later. The mouse runs in from the narrow end, tempted by food. There is a small paddle that when touched, moves upwards, releasing a heavy block of wood that falls onto the mouse, crushing it.

It was cheap to employ children to scare off birds with the noise produced by easily made wooden bird scarers, most of which continued in use into the early twentieth

French scarecrow dressed as an English bowman. Note rags tied to strings to scare birds. (Wiki Commons)

Bird sacring, Ripple church misericorde. One man is waving his hood and what may be a flag on a staff or a stylised wooden rattle.

century. They were often depicted with lepers, who were obliged to warn people of their approach. Wooden rattles were easy to make and cheap and not everybody could afford a bell. The exception with birds were the Lord's doves, which were allowed to eat what they wished. There were fines for killing them.

One of the earliest pictures of a scarecrow is found in a French manuscript, where the scarecrow is dressed as an English longbow archer. Nearby, strings with rags or feathers attached, have been stretched above the soil, much the same way as can be seen on many modern allotments.

Slings were easy and cheap to make and could be used for scaring off birds, even if killing them was more difficult. The *Luttrel Psalter* shows a man with a sling to scare off the birds following behind a harrow. Bows and crossbows would be more accurate than a sling at close range. At Ely it was recorded that birds were caught with traps, nets and birdlime; there is plenty of evidence to show that these methods were widely used.

The *Luttrel Psalter* shows a man trying to catch a bird using a net on a long pole, with a string to close the top. Several manuscripts show people catching birds with two long sticks that are held apart with a piece of wood that is attached to a cord. Some people are hiding in bushes and some pictures show another bird pegged to the ground to attract more down to the trap. Presumably if the bird alights on the sticks the string is pulled, and the bird is caught by the legs.

There was a trap to catch lots of birds at once, that is often illustrated and also described by Crescenzi. This form of trap is called a Clap Trap, and it operates like two hands clapping together. Similar traps are still used today, especially by ornithologists to capture larger birds so that they can be ringed. Two nets tied to

wooden poles are set out side by side and pegged to the ground at the corners. A cord is run around them. A bird can be pegged to the ground as a lure to attract other birds, or food can be spread instead. When there are enough birds a string can be pulled, causing the nets to be pulled upwards, enclosing the birds.

A less time consuming method would be to cover fruit trees and vegetables with nets to prevent the birds eating them.

Medieval Clap Trap used for catching several birds at once. (Wiki Commons)

More unusual is the illustrated manuscript showing a man shooting at birds in trees with a blowpipe.

Birdlime is a sticky glue-like substance made by boiling holly bark. It could be painted onto branches to catch birds. Caged birds can be placed to encourage other birds to fly down to perch on the branches. Simple bird traps could be made using an upturned basket resting on a small stick. Grain could be placed under the basket as bait. A length of string was attached to the stick. A person could hide and wait for the birds to eat the grain and then pull away the support, trapping them underneath. Alternatively, a simple arrangement of sticks could act as a trigger to cause the basket to fall. Pheasants were recorded as being caught using this method, by placing a small mirror under the basket to entice them in. At Higham Ferrers, William Newell was paid 3d to set up, 'an engine', on the Great Barn to scare off the crows, but there is no description of how it worked. It may have been a windmill with a clacker to make a lot noise.

Sometimes, a little divine intervention may be required to keep pests under control. One of the most terrible things that could happen to a medieval person was to be excommunicated from the protection and comforts of the church. This punishment was not just reserved for people, it could be used to clear pests. In 1120, a plague of caterpillars and field mice was destroying crops in his diocese, so the Bishop of Laon excommunicated them. The same thing happened again in 1480, when the inhabitants of Mossy and Pernan complained to the Spiritual Court of Autun about a plague of caterpillars. The court ordered priests to excommunicate the caterpillars and to repeat this until the caterpillars either died or went away. In 1481 and 1487 at Macon it was the turn of the snails to be excommunicated. Rats also suffered the wrath of the church, not only through excommunication, but there survives an English fifteenth century curse that will hopefully drive them go away.

A curse for rats
I command that all the rats that are here about,
That not one shall dwell in this place, within nor without,
Through the virtue of Jesus Christ, that Mary bore about,
To whom all creatures that owe reverence,
And through the virtue of Mark, Matthew, Luke and John –
All four gospels agree together
Through the virtue of Saint Gertrude, that pure maiden,
God grant that grace,
That no rats dwell in this place
That here especially were mentioned;
And through the virtue of Saint Kasi,
That holy man, that prayed to God almighty
For damage that they (the rats) did to his meadows

By day and by night.
God bade them flee and gone out from every man's sight.
Dominus Deus Sabaot! Emmanuel, the great God's name!
I commit this place from rats and all other shame.
God save this place from all other wicked creatures.
Both by day and by night!
Et in nomine Patris, et Filii et Spiritus Sancti.

Plant Diseases

For most plant diseases, there was little a medieval gardener could do other than pull up the affected plants and burn them to prevent the infection spreading.

Diseases in people were said to be caused by an imbalance of the four liquids, the humours, inside the body. The same theory was applied to animals and plants. One manuscript says that:

> 'If an apple tree begins to rot, or if the apples become rotten, then it is a sign that the bark of the tree is sick, and therefore cut it with a knife, and let it be opened, and when the humours thereof somewhat be flown out, let dung him well, and stop again the opening with clay.'

There was little a medieval gardener could do to control fungal disease such as coral spot, except remove the wood and burn it.

CHAPTER 12

The Medieval Gardening Year

ietro Crescenzi included a Calendar of Work in his book, so that the landowner or his agent could ensure that the land was being properly maintained and all tasks were being carried out at the correct times. The calendar mostly refers to the productive estate rather than the pleasure garden, but many tasks are similar, and we can deduce the order of events and the timing, making allowances for different countries and climates.

The calendar outlines the tasks that need carrying out and tells you when to do them. One advantage of the calendar is that you do not have to thumb through the whole book each time you want advice; you can just check the calendar for a quick reminder. I have combined several sources to produce this calendar.

The tasks have been edited because some of them would not have been appropriate to Britain. Allowance must be made for the different climate, but the processes are much the same.

Tasks for January

- Make gardens and dig the soil if it is not too wet or frozen. Dig around trees.
- Cut willows, rushes and poles for the vines.
- Sorrel and basil can be sown in January and February and as late as March at the waning of the moon. If you have to transplant them, make sure that there is as much soil as possible around the roots. Plant sage, lavender, dittany, mint and clary sage.
- In the soil that has been prepared sow vetches, beans and other herb seeds.
- In winter you should cut off the dead branches of sage plants.
- Transplant service trees, peaches, walnuts and almonds.
- Graft trees.
- Cut down the trees needed to build wooden structures and all sorts of trees for firewood to keep you warm.
- You can smoke the vines and cut them. The smoking is to kill insect pests.

Cutting firewood and tying brushwood in bundles to make faggots. (Getty Image)

- As it does not matter what the weather is like, you can make useful containers, carts, handcarts, and anything else that is necessary for the household.
- In mild places you can build farms and houses.
- Buy domestic animals and catch wild animals and move the bees.

Tasks for February

- The winter weather of December and January kills the pottage herbs and greens, that is to say, everything that is above ground, but in February the roots will grow fresh and tender leaves again as the frost finishes, and a fortnight later there will be spinach.
- Spinach comes in February and has a long crenelated leaf like an oakleaf and grows in bunches.
- Begin sowing garlic and leek seeds around Valentine's day. The leaves of the onions that are being grown to produce seed must not fall over and touch the ground and must be supported with ash forks. The seed will be black within the balls of dried flowers at Lammas of St Peter. The seeds should be dried on a cloth in the sun. Lammas commemorates the release of Peter from prison and is generally said to be the first day of August.
- Summer savoury and marjoram have similar flavours. They should be sown at the waning of the moon and will sprout after eight days.

- Savoury lasts only until St John's Day, 24 June.
- In the waning of the moon you should plant trees and vines. It is a good time to sow cabbages.
- Plant sage, lavender, dittany, mint, clary.
- If the soil is not too dry, nor too loose, make gardens. Plough and dig.
- Sow and plant all good herbs such as garlic, orache, aniseed, celery, beet, beans, basil, cabbage, onion, fennel, liquorice, lettuce, mint, leeks, poppy, parsley and shallots.
- Plant vines and vine cuttings. Buy vine roots. Buy rods for tying the vines.
- Peacocks, geese, hens and pigeons begin to stir up towards the end of the month.
- Buy honeybees and smoke them several times to clean them of all corruption and kill their king.
- During this month you can profitably buy sheepfolds, cowsheds, pigsties and stables. It is a good time to make rabbit warrens and fishponds for the fish.

Tasks for March

- There will be few green leaves at this time of the year. New nettle shoots and other wild plants would have been a blessing.
- At the wane of the moon you should graft. Plant houseleeks from March to St John's Day. Plant sage, lavender, dittany, mint and clary.
- Parsley sown on the eve of Lady Day will be above the soil in nine days.
- Parsley can be sown in March and be cut three times during the season. Don't transplant parsley because the plants will be poor but grown from seed you would have good plants. Do not let your parsley grow too tall.
- Plant fennel and marjoram at the waning moon. Marjoram prefers a richer soil than violets and if it grows in too much shade the leaves will turn yellow. When marjoram has produced a lot of shoots, you can take it up in tufts and replant it in pots.
- Violets and gillyflowers can be sown in March. When the frosts draw near, you should plant them in pots, when the moon is waning, so you can keep them under cover and protect them from cold in a cellar. During the day, set them in the open air in the sun, and water them at such time that the water may be drunk up and the earth is dry, before you set them under cover again, because they should never be wet when you put them away in the evening.
- Plant beans and break the first shoot by raking them, this encourages more shoots and thus more beans.
- At the waning moon you should plant trees and vines. Dig around tree bases.

Workers stake and tie vines. (Getty Image)

- March is also the time to begin growing cabbages. Sow in March for Lent; May for summer, July for harvest time and November for the winter. The ground must be well dug with manure stirred in before sowing the seeds. Four weeks later the plantlets should be transplanted into the dunged soil, and two weeks later they will be ready for pulling as young greens. In Galicia, northern Spain, the rural gardens still grow very tall kale-like cabbages which are used to make the local soup.
- In temperate places, plough the fields thoroughly in March. Hoe the wheat and barley.
- You can sow motherwort and hemp and onions.
- Decant the wine when the north wind blows. Cook the weak and thin wines to best preserve them, so they do not become pungent or sour.

Tasks for April

- Plant sage, lavender, dittany, mint, clary.
- In this month you must take care of all the trees and all the other plants and check that the bugs have not started to attack them.
- It will be necessary to water seeds and transplants.

- John Gardener wants plants for the cooking pot and medicine. He sows most of his seeds, including onions, in April. At this point he abandons the reader and gives no more gardening advice until September.
- Scare birds away from crops. This would have usually been children's work.
- In warm areas, you can shear the sheep and the early lambs and the horses and donkeys and their females.
- You must kill the butterflies that are plentiful when the violets flower; probably cabbage white butterflies.

Tasks for May

- May is the time for weeding and tending the young plants. Use mattocks, weeding hooks and your hands to remove weeds.
- Plant sage, lavender, dittany, mint, clary.
- Sow coriander, artichokes and purslane.
- Remove cabbage leaves with caterpillars. Keep the vines continually hoed. You must also disbud them. This encourages fewer but larger grapes.
- Remove cabbage leaves with caterpillars. Sprinkle ashes underneath the leaves and the caterpillars will die when it rains.

Tasks for June

- Weed all the crops.
- We can now enjoy our earlier hard work. Pick roses and strawberries. The pottage herbs will be producing rapidly in a good year and there will be plenty of greens to eat.
- Prepare the soil surface; it must be perfectly cleaned of all straw and hay and be manured and crumbled.

June was the month for enjoying the garden. A lady makes a rose chaplet amidst the bright flowers. (Getty Image)

- You should harvest the barley and the corn. Harvest the vegetables. Water beans at the full moon. Dig up broad beans at the waning of the moon.
- If the pears and apples are too heavy for the branches prop the ranches or remove some of the fruit, which seems rather early for modern fruit growers, but these instructions come from Italy.
- You can take off the honey from the hives if there is enough; you take the honey and the wax. In this month, the new bees leave; the master must shut the hive with diligence and skill so that they can't fly away, most of all up to nearly two or three hours to afternoon and have all the new hives ready to be gathered.

Tasks for July

- Harvest herbs. Mow the fields. Scythe grass before the dog days arrive.
- In July, the harvested fields can be ploughed for the second time. In temperate places, you can finish harvesting the wheat and picking the vegetables that have not already gone over.
- Weed the young vines in the morning and evening when the heat has dropped.

Harvesting herbs.

Tasks for August

- August is the best time to sow parsley because it will not grow high and will be good to use for the rest of the year. Keep the parsley free of weeds and remove the stones.
- Sow hyssop and cabbages for Easter. When the cabbages look like little crosses you can transplant them.
- In August the fields will be ploughed for the third time.
- Dig up the flax and the hemp when it begins to glow ripe in the heat.
- Harvest and dry gourds. Line them with gummy pitch and allow it to dry. You can then keep wine and other liquids in them. Gourds were the traditional water containers for pilgrims to Santiago de Compostela.
- Towards the end of the month, prepare everything that will be needed for the grape harvest.
- You can destroy the weeds and bracken by frequent ploughing.

Tasks for September

- John Gardener tells us that to grow saffron, we must have well manured soil. We should plant the corns using a dibber that is blunt and great, three days before Saint Mary's day, (September 8), but the next week will still be ok.
- Plant roses, peony, lily, dragonwort and currant bushes after the Nativity of Our Lady, September 8.
- Stop cutting the pottage herbs and greens in mid-September. Sow more cabbages.
- Dig out the bad weeds especially those with large leaves and firm roots.
- Towards the start of the month thin the leaves of the vines and after the middle of the month begin the grape harvest.
- The month of September is particularly recommended to make cisterns, water channels and wells.
- During this month you can easily catch quail and partridge with a sparrow hawk.

Tasks for October

- Manure the soil.
- Transplant leeks.
- Sow violets and gillyflowers on St Remy's Day, October 28.

- In temperate places sow bread wheat, rye, barley and flax.
- Pick the grapes that were not harvested in September.
- Clean out the streams and ditches.
- Plant cherries, apples, pears, and other trees that can withstand the cold.

Tasks for November

- Cut and prune the medlars and quinces. NB. Medlars bleed a sticky white sap if pruned when in active growth. In Britain it would be best to prune the medlars in early spring before the plant begins to grow again.
- Plant vines.
- Sow beans if the weather is warm.
- Sow flax.
- Transplant cabbages up to All Saints Day. If caterpillars have eaten the leaves and leave only veins, dig up the cabbage and plant deep to the top eye. Those with no leaves at all should be left as they will form sprouts.
- Transplant leeks.
- Sow prune stones whichever part of the country you are in.
- Cut wood for building when the moon is waning. This was because it was believed the wood would be drier than during a waxing moon when the moon was believed to make the sap to rise into the wood.
- Feed the pigs. Gather firewood.
- During this month you can catch different wild beasts, birds and fish.

Tasks for December

- In December you can sow broad beans that will shoot after the winter.
- From the season of All Saints we may sow beans, but to reduce the risk of them being caught by frost you should plant them around Christmas, and again in January, February and at the beginning of March. Plant them at different times, so that if some are damaged by frost, others will not be. When they come up out of the ground, as soon as they have six leaves you should spread earth over them and of them all, the first that ripen are the most delicate and they must be eaten the day they are shelled, or they may become black and have a bitter taste. This is a method still used by some modern gardeners as covering with earth protects young shoots from the cold and may encourage more stems.
- Prune the superfluous wood of trees and of hedges for burning.
- Cut poles and posts and prepare them to make stakes for the vines.

- Cut willows and rushes for tying the vines to their supports. Cut willow withies to make baskets, cages and other things.
- Dig dry ditches.
- During this month you can catch wild beasts by different means, especially with dogs when it snows.
- Catch birds with the help of tame birds, with several sorts of traps and bird lime.
- This is a good time to cut wood for carpentry, such as for buildings and other works.
- December is the time of celebration and Yule feasting. Animals will need to be tended but there will be little else to do. Ploughing will not begin again until Plough Monday, the first Monday after Epiphany, when the village priest will bless the ploughs.
- Crescenzi's book guides you through the gardening year, but for all his advice, he knows that things may not go according to plan. His book is concluded with a prayer:

'We pray to God, the Sovereign Lord, that by his grace and will and the help of Saint Peter, we shall be carried to his highest throne in paradise, with the help of his sweetest mother, the most glorious Queen, and of my Lord, Saint Denis. Amen.'

December was a time for feasting for some people. (Getty Image)

CHAPTER 13

Making your own Medieval Garden

Creating your own medieval garden is fairly easy. A few medieval features would not look out of place in a modern garden and could easily be fitted into even a small garden. Most of the materials can be bought at a garden centre.

A fountain or some sort of water feature is a must and is not difficult to install. Reconstituted stone containers are reasonably cheap, but a plastic container can be painted with a textured outdoor wall paint to make it appear to be stone. Mains electric pumps will give a good fountain jet of water, but if you are happy with a less powerful water jet, solar powered fountains are a good alternative. Water and electric make a potentially lethal mix so ensure that the pump is correctly installed by a qualified electrician.

Raised beds can easily be made using recycled wood. The wood can be supported with external or internal pegs hammered securely into the ground. If you can obtain willow or hazel withies, you could use them to weave around the edges of raised beds; there are many instructions on the internet. Many garden centres sell short sections of ready-made low wattle fencing, but it is better to make your own as it will be much sturdier. If making raised beds is too difficult, you could simply cut out square beds in a lawn.

You could allow the grass of your lawn to grow a little longer than usual and plant it with plugs of wildflowers to make a small flowery mead; sowing wildflower seeds directly onto the established turf rarely produces a good result. Allow the plants to set seed before cutting the grass. Plant plugs or sow seed of Yellow Rattle, a plant that is a parasite of grass. The grass will lose its vigour, allowing the wildflowers to withstand the competition.

Most of the plants for a medieval garden can be grown from seed or bought from a garden centre, although you need to buy some of the more unusual plants from a specialist herb nursery. If you are growing the plants for your own enjoyment, you can grow modern cultivars and you may prefer to use modern roses for a longer flowering period. Culinary herbs can be grown in a bed close to the kitchen or in pots that you can keep outdoors or even in the kitchen window. Planting herbs with scented leaves or flowers near a door, or next to a path or seating area is always a good idea in any garden. Many of the plants will attract insects into the garden, so you are helping the environment as well as making your own paradise garden, especially if you resist the urge to use insecticides and weed killers.

A grape vine can be grown as a bush in a pot or be trained against a wall or over a small arbour, and if you choose a good variety, you may even have enough grapes to make your own wine, but if not, you can eat them off the vine or juice them for a refreshing drink. Modern fruit trees can be obtained on dwarfing rootstocks, so it is possible to have a fruit tree even in a small garden, and maybe a productive tree seat.

For a small garden, a tree seat could be planted with a tree such as a decorative Crab Apple or a Rowan which could be easily pruned to stop it becoming too large. The grass could be planted with small wildflowers.

One thing is important, make the time to sit in your garden to enjoy the scents and sounds.

A tree seat can be made to fit a small garden.

Conclusion

We have become jaded, accustomed as we are, to gardens that produce evergreen leaves and flowers and scent for most of the year. The flowering period for medieval gardens was short compared to modern gardens. To enjoy a medieval garden, we need to become as children and take delight in such simple pleasures as sitting in long grass, surrounded by wildflowers and the humming of industrious insects. Admire the colour and scent of a solitary flower as if for the first time. The effort will be well rewarded.

To understand medieval gardens, we must free our imagination to a time when life was physically tough, even for the wealthy. After the harshness of winter, when you had to wear your personal central heating, we must try to feel the joy that comes with springtime:

'Now welcome, Summer, with soft sun,
You have shaken off Winters weather,
And driven away the long dark nights.'

Primroses and the cuckoo herald the start of warmer weather; the coming of summer with her mantle of fresh greenery, bejewelled with flowers. We must also forget our modern expectations of richly coloured borders that last long into the autumn and enjoy a brief burst of colour and scent which passes all too quickly.

Music, games, plants and animals and birds made gardens a place for enjoyment. (Walters Image)

A GUIDE TO MEDIEVAL GARDENS

Even during the medieval period, poets recognised the brevity of the gardens being enjoyed at their best:

> 'Now withers the rose and the lily-flower,
> That once bore the sweetest of scents;
> In summer, that sweet time.'

The summer has passed, and the harvest must be gathered in, the autumn chill is in the air and soon we must make ourselves ready for the deprivations of winter. A medieval song laments the coming of winter:

> 'Merry it is,
> While summer lasts,
> With the birds' song.
> Oh, now the wind howls and blasts,
> And we have fierce weather.
> Oh! Oh! This night is so long!
> And I, with much wrong,
> Must sorrow and mourn and fast.'

Acknowledgements

Special thanks to the Dean and Chapter of Ely for use of the poem 'In praise of Little Downham', from their book, *Liber Eliensis: A History of the Isle of Ely from the Seventh Century to the Twelfth*, compiled by a Monk of Ely in the Twelfth Century, 9781843830153, Boydell Press (2005), Translated by Janet Fairweather.

And for more verses from:

'A Medieval View of Ely', Brother Gregory's praises of the Isle of Ely in his *Life and Miracles of Saint Ætheldreda*, I, vv 287–371, from Corpus Christi College, Cambridge, Manuscript 393, translated into English verse by Janet Fairweather. Saint Peter's-in-Ely, 2010.

Thank you to the Folio Book Society for allowing the quote from the French Dialogue book that appears in their version on *The Goodman of Paris*, p.13

Especial thanks to Janet Hays and Margaret Jones for encouragement and lots of editing advice.

Picture credits

Photographs are by the author unless otherwise stated.

Dyers Plants. Bolton Castle.
King John's Garden, Romsey.

All digital Getty images courtesy of the Getty's Open Content Program. All reproduction pottery was made by Trinity Court Potteries, UK.

Page 58. Tithe Map.
Name of archive: Northamptonshire Archives and Heritage Service
Name of collection: Westmorland Archive.
Reference: 622
Title of archive: M(A) Inc a
Date of archive: 10/01/2009

Bibliography

This book is intended for the general reader. Much of my research is held as notes from many different sources including emails with various experts and my own translations of original sources. The following are just a few of the books that I have been used over the years. Many international libraries have digitised medieval manuscripts and other materials, making it easy to study representations of medieval gardens. The texts of many of the romances and other poems are now available online.

The Gardens Trust website has an online list of articles previously published by the Garden History Society from the journals, including quite a few by John Harvey about medieval gardens. They can be read online via JSTOR. For further information, go to: http://thegardenstrust.org.

Amherst, Alicia, *A History of Gardening in England*, London, Bernard Quaritch, 15 Piccadilly, W, 1896.

Bourin, Jeanne, *La Rose et la Mandragore. Plantes et jardins médiévaux*, Editions François Bourin, France, 1990.

Cambornac, Michel, *Plantes et Jardins du Moyens Ages*, Hartmann Edition, Paris, 1998.

Cato, *De Agricultura*, Andrew Dalby trans., Prospect Books, 1998.

Crisp, Sir Frank, *Illustrations of some Medieval Gardens, and of a few Tudor, Elizabethan, and Stuart Gardens, in which some of the Characteristics of Medieval Gardens are found, part II*, 4th edition, 1914.

Crisp, Sir Frank, *Mediaeval Gardens, 'Flowery Medes' and other arrangements of Herbs, Flowers and Shrubs grown in the Middle Ages, with some account of Tudor, Elizabethan and Stuart Gardens, Volumes One and Two*, John Lane the Bodley Head Limited, London, 1924.

Harvey, John, *Medieval Gardens* Batsford,1981. No longer in print.

Landsberg, Sylvia, *The Medieval Garden*, British Museum Press, 1995.

Brown Peter, Peter King and Paul Remfry, *Whittington Castle. The Marcher Fortress of the Fitz Warin Family*, Referee version, 2003.

McClean Teresa, *Medieval English Gardens*, Barrie and Jenkins, London, 1989.

Power, Eileen, *The Goodman of Paris (Le Ménagier de Paris) a Treatise on Moral and Domestic Economy by a Citizen of Paris c. 1393*, The Folio Society, 1992.

Searle, Eleanor, and Ross, Barbara, *Accounts of the Cellarers of Battle Abbey 1275–1513*, Sydney University Press, 1967.

Strabo, Walafrid, *Hortulus*, Raef Payne trans., the Hunt Botanical Library, Pennsylvania, 1966.

Sur la terre, comme au ciel, Éditions de la Réunion des Musées Nationaux, 2002.

Cornish Archaeology Journal, No.33, 1994.

Nassington Geophysical Survey Report 2003/33, GSB Prospection Ltd., Thorton, Bradford, 2003.

Medieval Gardens to visit

To see modern medieval style gardens in full bloom, the best time to visit is usually late May to mid-July. It is best to contact the site to find out how the garden is flowering because the weather and the local climate can make a great difference to when plants are in flower and the garden will be at its peak.

The information was correct when the book was printed.

Enjoy the pleasures of the medieval gardens at King John's House, Romsey and at many other sites.

Bodiam Castle, Bodiam, Robertsbridge, East Sussex, TN32 5UA.
A superb setting for a small medieval garden designed to show the many medieval uses of plants.
Web: www.nationaltrust.org.uk/bodiam-castle
Email: bodiamcastle@nationaltrust.org.uk
Tel: 01580 830 196

Bolton Castle, Nr Leyburn, North Yorkshire, DL8 4ET.
The castle has wonderful views. The herb garden contains over fifty varieties of culinary and medicinal herbs. There is a vineyard and a bowling green surrounded by flowers and shrubs which were found in this country before 1600. Some of the rises in the Rose Garden are medieval ones.
Web: www.boltoncastle.co.uk
Email: info@boltoncastle.co.uk
Tel: 01969 623 981

Bradwell Abbey, Alston Dr, Stacey Bushes, Milton Keynes MK13 9AP.
A small garden growing plants that could have been grown by the monks. Little remains of the abbey, but the small pilgrim chapel is well worth a visit. The garden is usually open during daylight hours.
Web: www.mkcdc.org.uk
Email: director@mkcdc.org.uk
Tel: 01908 227 229

Castle Acre Priory, Priory Rd, Castle Acre, King's Lynn, PE32 2XD.
Extensive ruins of a Cluniac monastery with a good exhibition about the site. The herb garden has plants that the monks may have grown. Castle Acre has a castle site, and the town gate house and part of the town walls survive.
Web: www.english-heritage.org.uk/visit/places/castle-acre-castle-acre-priory
Tel: 01760 755 394

Chichele College, College St, Higham Ferrers, Rushden NN10 8DZ.
A garden created by Northamptonshire Gardens Trust. There is a selection of medieval period plants that are grown in a raised bed and two long beds. English Heritage placed restrictions on the work that could be carried out to ensure that there would be no damage to any remaining archaeology beneath the soil; this meant that no more than four trees were allowed to be planted. Free admittance at any reasonable hour.
Web: www.chichelegarden.co.uk

More information at: www.highamferrerstourism.org.uk www.facebook.com/highamferrerstourism

N.B. There are no telephone or email contacts.

Queen Eleanor's Garden, Stony Stratford.

The garden commemorates the resting of the Queen Eleanor's coffin at Stony Stratford after her death in 1290, on her journey from Lincolnshire to Westminster Abbey. The plants are those that Eleanor would have known. Surrounding and sheltering the garden and the seats is a hedgerow of eglantine roses and hawthorn. The garden is on the triangle of grass at the North end of Stony Stratford at the junction of Queen Eleanor Street and the High Street, just before the bridge leading into Old Stratford.

Web: https://stonyinbloom.wixsite.com/stonyinbloom

N.B. There are no phone or email contacts for the garden.

Saint Mary de Haura, Church Street, Shoreham-by-Sea, Sussex, BN43 5DQ.

There are two small gardens in the churchyard not far from the West Door. There is a Mary Garden on the north side with plants symbolic of Mary. To the south is a garden dedicated to healing plants that may have been used medicinally by the Knights of the Order of St John of Jerusalem, otherwise known as the Hospitallers, who had a site in New Shoreham. The gardens contain a good selection of period plants.

Web: www.stmarydehaura.org.uk

E-mail: info@stmarydehaura.org.uk

Tel: 01273 440 202

Gainsborough Old Hall, Parnell Street, Gainsborough, Lincolnshire, DN21 2NB.

A garden area of raised beds with a wide selection of plants is near the main entrance. The site is now run by English Heritage.

Web: www.english-heritage.org.uk/visit/places/gainsborough-old-hall/

Email: No details available.

Tel: 01427 677 348

Glastonbury Abbey, Magdalene Street, Glastonbury, Somerset, BA6 9EL.

Within the grounds of the ruined abbey, where it is claimed that King Arthur was buried, there is a fairly large garden area dedicated to the plants that were grown during the medieval period, with an orchard and a wildlife pond.

Web: www.glastonburyabbey.com

Email: info@glastonburyabbey.com

Tel: 01458 832 267

King John's House, Church Street, Romsey, Hampshire, SO51 8BT.
King John's House dates from the thirteenth century and first belonged to Romsey Abbey until its dissolution in 1539. The south side of the garden is laid out in a series of gardens with a medieval style herber and a series of beds with flowers of the period. The north side of the garden is more informal, having an area of spring meadow planted with apple trees, a summer meadow and bounded on one side by a stream. There is also a stone paved courtyard with a quince and a pentise which provides a shady seating area.
Web: www.kingjohnshouse.org.uk
Email: deputymanagerkjh@aol.com
Tel: 01794 512 200

Lavenham Guild Hall, Market Place, Lavenham, Sudbury, Suffolk, CO10 9QZ.
The Guildhall of Corpus Christi is a beautiful timber-framed building. There is a small garden with plants that were used to dye cloth.
Web: www.nationaltrust.org.uk/lavenham-guildhall
Email: lavenhamguildhall@nationaltrust.org.uk
Tel: 01787 247 646

Michelham Priory, Upper Dicker, Hailsham, East Sussex, BN27 3QS.
The recreated medieval gardens include the *Hortus Conclusus* and a pleasure garden. The cloister garden is situated on the site of Michelham Priory's original cloister. It is divided into quarters around a well, with a flowery mead which is surrounded with medieval plants, including roses, Madonna lilies, columbines and vegetables for pottage. There is a green oak tunnel arbour trained with grape vines. There is an apple orchard with mulberry, walnut, sweet chestnut and medlar trees planted nearby. The orchard is under-planted with naturalised daffodils for spring display and wildflowers for the summer. The physic garden has a collection of herbs for medicinal, culinary and utilitarian use, which would have been available to the Priory in the Middle Ages.
Web: www.sussexpast.co.uk/properties-to-discover/michelham-priory
Email: adminmich@sussexpast.co.uk
Tel: 01323 844 224

The Monk's Cell, Mount Grace Priory, Northallerton, North Yorkshire DL6 3JG.
The cell and garden have been restored to give an impression as to how a Carthusian monk could make use of his personal space. The garden is decorative and planted to show the different use of plants. The box hedges are not a feature of a medieval garden.
Web: www.english-heritage.org.uk/visit/places/mount-grace-priory
Email: yorkshire@english-heritage.org.uk
Tel: 01609 883 494

Prebendal Manor, Church Street, Nassington, Northamptonshire, PE8 6QG.
Many of the medieval garden features have been removed and some modern planting added to make the site a more desirable venue for weddings. It is still a wonderful site with views towards Fotheringhay Deer Park.
Web: www. prebendal-manor.co.uk
Email: info@prebendal-manor.co.uk
Tel: 01780 782 575

Queen Eleanor's Garden, The Castle, Winchester, Hampshire.
Created by Hampshire Gardens Trust, the garden accessed via the Great Hall. A small garden that makes good use of the space to show different garden features.
Web: www.hants.gov.uk/greathall/eleanor
Email: the.great.hall@hants.gov.uk
Tel: 01962 840 476

Reading Abbey, Abbey St., Reading RG1 3BA.
The home of the medieval song, *Sumer is icumen in*. The garden is set in the atmospheric ruins of the abbey. The garden is quite small, but there are plans to develop it.
Web: www.readingmuseum.org.uk   www.readingabbeyquarter.org.uk
Email: r.douglas@reading.ac.uk
Tel: 01189 373 400 extn.74977

Rye Castle Museum, Ypres Tower, Rye.
The medieval garden is in the courtyard which was once the exercise yard for prisoners. Although quite small, the garden has been carefully designed to make the best use of the space. A good selection of plants is planted in beds at the base of the walls with climbers trained up the walls on wooden trellis. There are raised beds in the centre of the courtyard and a seat and table sheltered by climbing plants. To cater for the taste of modern visitors, there are some no-period plants to extend the gardens' period of interest.
Web: www.ryemuseum.co.uk
Email: info@ryemuseum.co.uk
Tel: 01797 226 728

Shaftesbury Abbey, Park Walk, Shaftesbury SP7 8JR.
The herb beds are attractively arranged against the Abbey walls. There are also four large raised beds just outside the museum doors, so that everyone can enjoy the pleasure of these herbs. Each bed contains herbs traditionally used as utilitarian, the practical plants for dyeing and strewing, medicinal, culinary and religiously

symbolic plants linked to the Virgin Mary, such as roses, marigold and fleur de lys as
the Abbey was dedicated to her.
Web: www.shaftesburyabbey.org.uk
Email: office@shaftesburyabbey.org.uk
Tel: 01747 852 910

Settlers Garden, Stanwick Lakes, Wellingborough, Northamptonshire, NN9 6GY.
A community project to make a garden showing the different uses of plants during the
medieval period. Raised beds are enclosed with a fence. There is a small orchard next
to the garden. The garden is next to the Ancestral Barn, which was built by volunteers
using traditional methods. Admission free, but there is a charge for parking.
Web: www.nenesettlers.org
Email: Settlers@rftrust.org.uk
Tel: 01933 625 522

Sir Roger Vaughan's Garden, Tretower Court, Crickhowell, Powys, Wales.
Tunnel arbour covered with roses, honeysuckle and vines. Herber with chequerboard
beds around a water feature. Orchard areas include almond, quince, mulberry, wild
cherry, medlar and three cider apples. Elsewhere, a Brown Turkey fig and a Blenheim
Orange and a Cat's Head ('Duke of York') cooking apple.
Web: www.cadw.wales.gov.uk/default.asp?id=6&PlaceID=136
Email: tretowercourt@gov.wales
Tel: 01874 730 279

Tintagel Castle, Cornwall.
The remains of the small medieval garden are about 130m away from the inner ward
of the castle ruins, just beyond the remains of the chapel. The setting is very dramatic
and well worth a visit.
Web: www.english-heritage.org.uk/daysout/properties/tintagel-castle
Email: southwest@english-heritage.org.uk
Tel: 01840 779 084

Torre Abbey, The Kings Drive, Torquay, Devon, TQ2 5JE.
The garden with Turf Seats, willow tunnels and authentic planting is enclosed within
a wattle fence.
Web: www.torre-abbey.org.uk
Email: torreabbeyenquiries@torbay.gov.uk
Tel: 01803 293 593

Weald and Downland Museum, Singleton, Chichester, West Sussex, PO18 0EU.
There are two gardens based on medieval ideas. Bayleaf farmhouse has been set out to show a yeoman's property. The garden has a garden designed by Dr Sylvia Landsberg and created by R. Holman. The vegetable garden has cabbages and turnips, leeks or onions, peas and beans, lettuce, spinach beet and a wide selection of herbs. The orchard contains apple and pear trees. The garden is maintained as authentically as possible. Some distance away the Hangleton garden was designed as if it were the garden of a retired couple.
Web: www.wealddown.co.uk
Email: office@wealddown.co.uk
Tel: 01243 811 363

Whittington Castle, Whittington, Oswestry, Shropshire, SY11 4DF.
The castle grounds are always open. There is a tearoom and gift shop.
Web: www.whittingtoncastle.co.uk
E-mail: info@whittingtoncastle.co.uk
Tel: 01691 662 500

Winifred's Well, Woolston, Near Oswestry.
The property is maintained by the Landmark Trust. The well is usually accessible at any reasonable hour but be aware that people pay a lot of money to rent the property, so please respect their privacy.
Web: www.landmarktrust.org.uk
Email: info@landmarktrust.org.uk
Tel: 01628 825 920